T0328999

THE DARWIN COLLEGE LECTURES

These essays are developed from the 2010 Darwin College Lecture Series. Now running for twenty-five years, these popular Cambridge talks take a single theme each year. Internationally distinguished scholars, skilled as communicators, address the theme from the point of view of eight different arts and sciences disciplines.

Subjects covered in the series include

RISK

Recent events from the economic downturn to climate change mean that there has never been a better time to be thinking about and trying to better understand the concept of risk. In this book, prominent and eminent speakers from fields as diverse as statistics to classics, neuroscience to criminology, politics to astronomy, as well as speakers embedded in the media and in government, have put their ideas down on paper in a series of essays that broaden our understanding of the meaning of risk. The essays come from the prestigious Darwin College Lecture Series which, after twenty-five years, is one of the most popular public lecture series at the University of Cambridge. The risk lectures in 2010 were among the most popular yet and, in essay form, they make for a lively and engaging read for specialists and non-specialists alike.

RISK

Edited by *Layla Skinns, Michael Scott* and *Tony Cox*

CAMBRIDGE
UNIVERSITY PRESS

CAMBRIDGE
UNIVERSITY PRESS

University Printing House, Cambridge CB2 8BS, United Kingdom

Cambridge University Press is part of the University of Cambridge.

It furthers the University's mission by disseminating knowledge in the pursuit of education, learning and research at the highest international levels of excellence.

www.cambridge.org
Information on this title: www.cambridge.org/9780521171977

© Cambridge University Press 2011

First published 2011

A catalogue record for this publication is available from the British Library

Library of Congress Cataloguing in Publication data
Risk / edited by Layla Skinns, Michael Scott, Tony Cox.
    p.   cm. – (The Darwin College lectures ; 24)
Includes bibliographical references and index.
ISBN 978-0-521-17197-7 (pbk.)
1. Risk – Sociological aspects. 2. Risk perception.   3. Risk assessment.   I. Skinns, Layla.
II. Scott, Michael, 1981–   III. Cox, Tony, 1941–
HM1101.R548   2011
302'.12 – dc23   2011019857

ISBN 978-0-521-17197-7 Paperback

Contents

Figures

Tables

Acknowledgements

The Darwin College Lecture Series 2010, from which this collection of essays are taken, was conceived, developed and delivered with the help of many people. We are exceedingly grateful for all of their contributions, large or small. Thanks must be extended first of all to the contributors to the lecture series and to the book. Many thanks are also owed to Janet Gibson, whose work 'behind the scenes' meant there was a seamless transition between each of the different stages of the lecture series and the book. The support and commitment, but also the knowledge and experience of the Master and Vice-Master of Darwin College, William Brown and Andy Fabian, in translating the lecture series into a book were also central to its completion. For this we are truly grateful.

1 Introduction

LAYLA SKINNS, MICHAEL SCOTT AND TONY COX

The Darwin College Lecture Series

The chapters in this book originate from lectures given as part of the 2010 Darwin College Lecture Series on the subject of risk. This series constitutes one of Cambridge University's largest and longest-running set of public lectures. Begun in 1986, the Darwin College Lecture Series has, each year, focused on a single theme and invited eminent speakers from around the world to reflect on what that theme means in their field.[1] Over the last twenty-five years the chosen themes have ranged from survival to serendipity, conflict, power, structure, sound, evidence, evolution, the fragile environment, predicting the future, time and identity, reflecting many of the key issues that affect our local and global societies, as well as celebrating important milestones in our history. 'Origins' was the subject of the first Darwin College Lecture Series in 1986. 'Time' was chosen to commemorate the 2000 millennium series, and in 2009, the title of the series was 'Darwin', celebrating the anniversary of Charles Darwin by looking at his ideas and influence.

The cornerstones of the Darwin College Lecture Series, and the books which accompany them, are their interdisciplinary approach and target audience. In the book following the first Darwin College Lecture Series in 1986, D. H. Mellor, Vice-Master of Darwin College, put it like this:

> University research covers a great range of subjects. To try to comprehend all of them would be foolish: life is too short, and anyway no one is good at everything. But most subjects are to some extent spectator

[1] Further information about past and present lectures can be found on the Darwin College website. www.darwin.cam.ac.uk/lectures/.

1

sports. You needn't be a musician to appreciate some modern music – though no doubt it helps – nor a cosmologist to appreciate some modern cosmology. And many spectators have common interests in very different subjects ... there is, therefore, a predictable demand for a series of public lectures by leading authorities in interdisciplinary topics ... and not only for lectures: such interests are not confined to Cambridge, nor to any one year.[2]

Since 1986, each year, over the course of eight lectures, and in the corresponding written chapters, the chosen theme of the Darwin College Lecture Series is thus tackled by a number of experts in a wide range of subjects – the 2010 lectures covered everything from statistics to classics, neuroscience to criminology, government to astronomy and terrorism to news media. As a result, people coming to the lectures, and reading the resulting essays in this book, are treated to a rare opportunity to engage with a wide range of approaches and insights. At the same time, the lecture series is specifically aimed at engaging not just academics, but, just as importantly, a wide public audience. Each lecture and its corresponding chapter assumes no previous knowledge of the subject. In doing so, this series, over the last twenty-five years, has occupied an important place in the way in which Cambridge University reaches out to engage with the wider public on the issues that interest and confront us all.

It is fitting, therefore, that the Darwin College Lecture Series has also been at the forefront of the University's use of new technology to allow even greater access and engagement. In the past, that has meant helping to invest in the digital relay of the lectures to larger lecture theatres to cope with increasing audience numbers. But in recent years it has meant, just as importantly, making the lectures available to communities beyond Cambridge via the internet. For the past few years, the lectures have been accessible online as some of the University's most popular podcasts, and in 2010, for the first time, many of the lectures were available as both podcasts and videos, with more people able to follow the series on social networking sites such as Facebook and Twitter, where we posted regular updates about the series as it progressed. In producing the lectures and also the essays for this book, the contributors have thus been able to reflect not only on their own lecture, but to engage fully with the

[2] Mellor 1988: ix.

lectures of others in the series and with the feedback of a much wider audience from across the globe. The book, is, we feel, definitely the richer for it.

Risk in 2010

In conceiving the 2010 lecture series, each of the organisers brought their own ideas about the meaning of risk from their respective fields. In the field of criminology, for example, risk is a concept which has gained in importance, particularly over the last twenty years. A quick search of online criminological resources yields literally thousands of 'hits'. Risk has been thought of in a variety of ways. Since the pioneering Cambridge Study in Delinquent Development[3] – which has contributed to our understanding of 'criminal careers' across the life-course – there has been an interest in the 'risk factors' (as well as, more recently, the 'protective factors') that increase (or decrease) the chances of offending in terms of its onset, frequency, persistence or duration. These risk factors include things such as impulsiveness, coming from a large family where parents and/or siblings are convicted offenders, having a low income and living in socially disorganised neighbourhoods.[4] What are less understood, though, given their new form and focus, are the risk factors for would-be terrorists. Nevertheless, Lucia Zedner's thought-provoking chapter in this volume challenges us to think beyond merely what factors propel terrorists, towards a closer examination of the risks inherent in authoritarian governmental responses to them.

Risk is also something that needs to be assessed, managed and predicted by those working in the criminal justice system, including the police, probation and prison services. Risk assessment, involving both objective and subjective components, affects how prisoners are dealt with inside prison, whether and when they are released from prison and subsequently how they are managed by the probation service in the community. Paradoxically, through its imperfections, risk assessment is a 'risky business'. Tragic cases of dangerous offenders re-offending on their release into the community show the risk of 'false negatives', while prisoners detained

---

[3] Farrington 2007.   [4] Ibid.

for indefinite and lengthy periods of time contribute to the risk of 'false positives'.

Furthermore, the capacity for risk to permeate the operation of the criminal justice system has been captured in two influential criminological theories. The analytical lens of risk has been used to help us understand the way that offenders are punished. It is argued that punishment is no longer concerned with the rehabilitation and reform of individual offenders; rather, it is about the identification and management of categories of risk, which are thought about in ways similar to how risk is conceived of by the insurance industry.[5] The concept of risk has also been used to challenge the existing ways we understand the police, drawing on social theory about the 'risk society'.[6] The central argument is that, contrary to a conventional view of the police as maintaining social order, and defined by their capacity to use force in an unlimited array of circumstances, the police are primarily regarded as 'expert knowledge workers' engaged in the surveillance and management of a much wider range of risks than in the past, in conjunction with a loosely connected network of other organisations.[7]

Just as in criminology, interest in the concept of risk has been building over the last decades in the field of ancient history and archaeology. While it is often impossible, given the nature of the surviving evidence, to perform a meaningful statistical analysis of risks in the ancient world, it is possible to think about ways in which the ancients responded to the uncertainty of the world around them and conceived of ways to limit that risk and adapt to it. How much the modern word 'risk' (and its connotations) is applicable to ancient worlds is a topic Mary Beard returns to in her essay in this book. Most usually, such approaches have focused on how the ancients developed strategies in their domestic economy to cope with fluctuations in agriculture and food production – that is, to mitigate the risk of starvation and maximise the chance of survival.[8] But more recently the term has also been applied to the analysis of religious behaviour in ancient Greece, in particular of curse tablets. This fascinating source of evidence – lead tablets engraved with a curse by one person

[5] Feeley and Simon 1992 and 2003.   [6] Beck 1992.
[7] Ericson and Haggerty 1997.
[8] Cf. Gallant 1991; Garnsey 1988; Halstead and O'Shea 1989.

against another – have been found in different locations around Greece and relate to many areas of activity: business, law, the theatre and most especially to issues of love and marriage. It has been argued that they represent, in a world ruled by gods, attempts by individuals to harness the power of some of those gods to control the actions of others and thus reduce the risk they pose, or, alternatively, to take revenge on those people for the negative risks to which the curser has been exposed.[9] In the ancient cultures of Greece and Rome, risk has therefore been shown to be both a factor in the calculation of one of the most basic principles of humanity – survival – but also a very sophisticated concept to be moderated, controlled and utilised as part of the business of social interaction.

Research on the much longer geological time-scale of Earth's history shows that there have been many large and sometimes abrupt changes in the Earth's environment. The risks arising from these have threatened the survival, and affected the evolution, of the living world (the 'great extinctions'). In the shorter time-frame of recorded human history, there is much evidence (for example in religious beliefs, traditions, buildings and earthworks) of awareness of the threat of disaster from natural causes such as earthquakes, tempests, floods and volcanic eruptions, and of the steps taken to avoid harm to the community. Archaeological evidence from around the world indicates that such awareness was influential in the development of early human societies. But it is only in the modern age that humans have attempted to measure and predict such events, opening the prospect of reducing the risk of damaging impacts.

As the preceding discussion demonstrates, it is clear that risk is a topic of interest to contributors from a diverse range of disciplines, something which has been a primary concern of organisers of the Darwin College Lecture Series since its inception. Indeed, this was the reason risk was chosen rather than the topic of security, which was initially identified as a possible theme for the 2010 Lecture Series. Security may have had a broader meaning and more positive connotations, but was also more difficult to apply to disciplines in, for example, the natural sciences.

[9] Eidinow 2007.

More importantly, though, the lecture series was conceived, planned and finalised between April 2008 and December 2009, a period marked by uncertainties in the face of a worldwide economic downturn. It seemed like risk was all around us and, furthermore, that people were beginning to question how the realities of the risks we faced were being conveyed and understood, particularly through the media.[10] What better time, then, for a lecture series on this very topic? We hoped it might contribute to the debate and help the public to better understand what risk is and how it can be applied to a variety of areas, and offer a way of mitigating, not fuelling, public anxieties. Knowledge not ignorance can be a powerful tool enabling the public to move beyond being the passive victims that Mary Beard argues, in her essay in this book, are characteristic of contemporary risk societies.

Apart from this, risk is a topic deserving of academic and public attention in and of itself: it is an intriguing concept, difficult to define. The essays in this book show just how varied these definitions can be. For example, David Spiegelhalter defines it as 'anything to do with situations where "bad" (or "good") things may, or may not, happen', while Christopher Hood argues that the risk that matters most, at least in politics, is the risk of blame.

Moreover, risk is of cultural significance in contemporary society. It is a term that features regularly in public debates, not only about the economic downturn, but also about many other things, including health and safety, diet and public health, dangerous offenders, transport and the environment. Searching any online broadsheet newspaper under the term risk confirms this impression of how regularly the word features in newspaper articles and commentary by journalists and the public. Risk is furthermore of growing interest across academic disciplines, not just in criminology and ancient history. Consequently, we found that in the early stages of planning the lecture series, we had a number of potential topics and speakers to choose from. Of course, the obvious topic to select would have been risk and the economy, but we decided on other topics which were of equal importance culturally, socially, empirically and epistemologically, which would also provide the audience with context

---

[10] Gardner 2008.

and perhaps even with ways of better understanding the unfolding economic risks.

The lecture series led our audience from an understanding of key concepts to an examination of risk on individual, societal and global scales, schedules of speakers permitting. David Spiegelhalter's lecture was placed first to provide a clear definition of risk and therefore a firm foundation for what was to come. Before looking at risk on an individual level, the lecture took a slight detour from its unfolding sequence, thanks to the second lecture in the series by Ben Goldacre on risk, science and the media (not included in this volume). To explore risk and the individual, initially, we wanted to ask people who engaged in risky behaviour, such as mountaineering or ballooning or space travel, to talk about their personal experiences of risk, but to our surprise few of the people we approached viewed what they did as risky. Perhaps rationalising risk in this way is what enabled them to carry on doing these activities. Consequently, we took the opportunity to go beyond a person's experiences and look deep into their brain, which was the subject of the third lecture by John O'Doherty.

From this point onwards the lectures began to broaden their scope to take in risk on a societal scale. The fourth lecture in the series, by Christopher Hood, on risk and government, was followed by lectures on risk in the ancient world by Mary Beard, and by Lucia Zedner's lecture on risk and terrorism in the present. The final part of the lecture series explored risk in a global setting, focusing, in particular, on potentially catastrophic environmental issues. This global focus was enabled by Mark Bailey, who spoke about risk and asteroid strikes, and by Bob Watson talking about risk and climate change.

Internationally renowned speakers were selected because of their specialist knowledge and skills as communicators. Indeed, their reputations contributed to an extremely popular lecture series. For example, Ben Goldacre's lecture rivalled Desmond Tutu's held at the Cambridge Union (because of its larger capacity than the Lady Mitchell Hall) in 1994, as the most popular lecture in the twenty-five-year history of the series. With an audience of over a thousand, this meant that the Lady Mitchell Hall and the two overspill lecture theatres were completely full and the audience waited patiently, in spite of his slightly late arrival – with the latter being another first in the history of the series. Furthermore, the risk lectures seemed to capture the public's imagination. Their popularity might also have been because of our comprehensive approach to publicising them through traditional means such as the *Cambridge Evening News*, BBC Radio Cambridgeshire and student newspapers such as *Varsity*; mediums such as Facebook, Twitter and the newly established Cambridge University TV, whose staff interviewed most of our speakers; as well as by involving local people in the lecture series through events, which helped raise the profile of the lectures in the wider community in Cambridge.

Extending our reach in 2010

We wanted to ensure in 2010 that as wide an audience as possible was involved, not just in listening to the risk lectures, but also in putting forward their own understandings of risk through many different media. To that end, we approached art and film institutions across Cambridge to work with us on responding to the subject of risk. The results were impressive. Kettle's Yard organised its half-term art classes and its regular poetry classes for children around the subject of risk. Cambridge Film Consortium ran film classes on the theme. Sixth-form students at Long Road Sixth Form College and students from Anglia Ruskin University made short films about risk as part of their studies. In addition, the British Film Institute opened its archives to us to provide some fantastic examples of very early films reflecting our risk theme. All of these were incorporated into a video presentation shown before each of the lectures and made available online.

Responses ranged from a visual interpretation of risk as a dog coming perilously close to one's leg (shown in Figure 1.1) to a poem about risk in the twenty-first century, exploring the dangers of children using the internet unsupervised (shown in Figure 1.2), to clips of the first filmed ascent of Everest and a short film about the risk to one's personal life of being too passionate and engaged in one's work. Our thanks go to everyone who participated in this project. As a result of their work, we felt that not only were more people engaged in thinking about what risk meant to them, but, equally importantly, that we were all being encouraged to realise just how many different elements of our history

FIGURE 1.1 Drawing of dog by Kettle's Yard Saturday drawing class participant, autumn term 2009.

Risk A Verse

She lowers her Daily Mail,
Reaches for the Oxford marmalade;
'I'd never let mine
Play out,
Unsupervised'
She says,
'Un-sup-er-vised',
The syllables stretch,
As she teeters along her moral high wire.

Upstairs, her child
Runs
Deep into the dark
Of his very own wood;
He smiles.
Silently, a wolf slips
Through the black trees
Of the cyber forest,
Prowling.

Sophie Smiley, creative writing course,
Autumn 2009

FIGURE 1.2 Poem by Sophie Smiley, Kettle's Yard creative writing course, autumn 2009.

and lives revolve around the concept of risk and just how fragmented and diverse our understanding of risk can be. It confirmed once again how appropriate this topic was for the Darwin College Lecture Series and how much there was still to learn about it.

The chapters ahead

In Chapter 2, David Spiegelhalter explains with great clarity about quantifying uncertainty, with examples ranging from the election of Barak Obama to football odds to cycling. He begins by highlighting that while 'true risks' may be eclipsed by gut reactions, these may not suffice all the time, which is why we need a more systematic and analytical approach. He sets out how probabilities are allotted to events, how they can be represented and what these representations mean. For example, he explains about the quantification of small but lethal risks with the help of the 'friendly unit of deadly risk', the micromort, which represents a one-in-a-million chance of dying. The main argument in his essay, though, is that statistical models which attempt to quantify uncertainty are inherently subjective, as well as inaccurate due to 'unknowns' and, in the words of Donald Rumsfeld, the 'unknown unknowns'. And he suggests that public figures need to act with humility when communicating about these uncertainties.

Ben Goldacre's lecture was next in the 2010 series. In it, he implicitly addressed the risks associated with 'bad science', which is communicated to the public through the media. We briefly outline his lecture here, since he was unable to contribute an essay to the present book. In his lecture, he debunked stories in the press, ranging from the changing strength of cannabis, to the factors that improve school children's performance, to the links between mobile phone masts and suicide, and between MMR and autism. He persuasively argued that the media have deceived the public and have failed to uphold their end of the bargain, in terms of publishing stories that are factually accurate. Rather than relying on 'gold-standard' scientific evidence published by established academics, 'churnalists' have shown a preference for 'experts' who conduct research in their 'Shedquarters' or for the 'lab that always gives positive results' because, according to 'Goldacre's Law', there will always be one doctor somewhere in the world who is willing to defend any imaginable proposition, no matter how absurd. With his words 'it's always more complicated than you think' he clearly articulated that scientific stories in the media, and scientific research, more generally require careful scrutiny.

In Chapter 3, John O'Doherty, who gave the third lecture in the series, provides an insight into how we reach decisions under conditions of uncertainty, and the importance of the ventromedial prefrontal cortex in performing these tasks. He examines research from 'neuroeconomics', in which neuroscientists have begun to integrate economic theories about rational actors (weighing up the costs and benefits of their actions to maximise pleasure and minimise pain) with neuroscientific methods in which the brain is scanned while participants engage in decision-making tasks. In this chapter he examines a number of studies from this nascent field, which have looked at things such as performance on bandit-machines or experiments involving food smells and the attractiveness of people's faces in the brains of the impaired and non-impaired, all of which have been used to understand more about decision-making under conditions of uncertainty. Importantly, though, he argues that different areas of the brain are stimulated in individuals who exhibit risk-taking behaviour than in those who are risk-averse.

In Chapter 4, Christopher Hood argues that government responses to a variety of risks are structured, in part, by the need to avoid blame. Blame, he argues, is made up of perceptions of the level of harm caused and of who is responsible, and asserts that government officials employ three main strategies to avoid blame. Firstly, they attempt to deflect blame, although this may not be fully achievable. Secondly, public officials diminish perceptions of harms, and their own responsibility for them, through complex partnership arrangements which enable responsibilities to be buck-passed from one governmental agency to another. Thirdly, with the help of spin-doctors and PR companies, government officials are able to weasel their way out of blame through 'presentational strategies'. Perhaps the most interesting part of his argument is that blame-avoidance need not be seen as altogether negative. Rather, he suggests that blame-avoidance can promote social restraint and observance of the rules. He argues, finally, that the crux of the matter is being able to distinguish between the 'good' and 'bad' types of blame-avoidance and, in this regard, political processes and not the law should play a role in promoting the 'good' and discouraging the 'bad'.

Chapter 5 comes from Mary Beard's lecture, which was the fifth in the series. In her chapter she draws a distinction between the ancient model of danger and contemporary sociological understandings of the modern risk society. In the risk society, she argues, hazards are given an arithmetic value, based on probabilities, and the state is regarded as responsible for managing these risks, placing citizens in the position of passive victims. By contrast, in the ancient world, she suggests, Roman understandings of risk were not based on probabilities, since this was only recognised later, in the sixteenth century. Moreover, she argues that the Romans actively engaged with risks, living in what she calls an 'aleatory society', with the attitude of *alea iacta est*, which she suggests should be translated as 'let the dice be thrown'. That is, the Romans looked danger in the eye, rather than being the playthings of fate (which the usual translation as 'the die is cast' tends to imply). In addition, she argues that this Roman understanding of danger can speak to contemporary societies in which people, including academics and researchers, have become fearful and passive victims of risk.

The essay that constitutes Chapter 6 is by Lucia Zedner and is on risk and terrorism. She begins by examining how difficult it is to assess such risks, given that the data are unreliable and human behaviour is less amenable to quantification than are phenomena in the natural sciences, meaning greater reliance on subjective professional judgement – made all the more difficult because of the politically charged nature of terrorism. Importantly, she also notes that while the UK has faced terrorist threats in the past, the 'new terrorism', as she calls it, is qualitatively different in view of its global scale, its novel rules and tactics (e.g. suicide bombers) and its association with ideologies about jihad. She goes on to say that the actual risk of being a victim of a terrorist attack is relatively small, no greater than drowning in the bath, for example. What makes the risk so potent, though, is the deliberateness of the acts and the scale of the harm caused. Yet there is also a set of 'countervailing risks', she argues, such as radicalisation, as well as 'collateral risks' to human rights and the rule of law as the state exercises ever-increasing power over citizens (for example through identity cards). She ends the essay on a note of hope, however, offering ideas about 'resilience strategies', which involve communities and the judiciary and which could help us to 'live with risk but without terror'.

In Chapter 7, Mark Bailey writes about the risks faced on Earth from Near-Earth Objects (NEOs), which include comets, asteroids and fragments of them. He argues that these outer-space risks trump other kinds of natural catastrophes simply because they could bring about the extinction of the species, as was the case for the dinosaurs 65 million years ago. He describes some of the 'dark skies' research, from astronomy, which has been used to quantify the risks that NEOs pose. For example, this research has concluded that there are around 1,000 NEOs with diameters larger than 1 km in our solar system which could collide with Earth once every 200,000 years, making such an event unlikely. However, the level of harm that NEOs could cause, whether the obliteration of an entire country or a tsunami or an irrevocable alteration of the climate of the planet, leads him to ask whether NEOs are something that we can safely ignore or whether we should take the long view of them. Moreover, he argues that the level of harm that asteroids could cause means that mitigating the risk of asteroid strikes is a political task of global proportions.

In the final chapter, Bob Watson argues that there is no doubt that the Earth's temperature is increasing, the last decade being the warmest of all, and little doubt that this increase is in part a result of human activity, with the emission of gases such as carbon dioxide, nitrous oxide, methane and sulphur into the atmosphere. While it is difficult to predict precisely the likely increase in the temperature of the Earth, he argues that by 2090 we could see an increase of 2–3°C, but it is more likely to be around 3–4°C, and even 4–5°C. He argues that such an increase in the Earth's temperature could seriously threaten the security of food and water, as well as biodiversity, particularly in sub-Saharan Africa. He goes on to make a powerful case for a drastic de-carbonising of the atmosphere through technological changes (for example greater use of renewable energy sources), policies on energy pricing (e.g. a higher price for carbon), but, more importantly, through long-term international legally binding regulatory frameworks with an equitable allocation of responsibilities between the major emitters of carbon dioxide. It also requires, so he argues, regulation (not education or persuasion) of individuals who care little about climate change and the collective will of society.

As this brief summary shows, risk was perfectly suited to the inter-disciplinary nature of the Darwin College Lecture Series and, judging by the level of interest from start to finish, the 2010 series seemed also to capture the public's imagination. Needless to say, we were delighted with its success and this book is a welcome addition, which puts contributors' words on paper and draws the 2010 lecture series to a close.

Risk beyond 2010

The lecture series may have ended, but we believe that the issues it raised, and which are explored in more detail in this book, have greater longevity. As the lectures were unfolding, the political storm around the University of East Anglia's Climate Change Unit was gathering force, focusing national interest on the veracity of statistics about the risks we face in the future in relation to global warming. Indeed, it is perhaps in how we face up to the risks around us, and go about quantifying, explaining and dealing with those risks, that we believe this series of lectures and essays has the most to offer to the wider debate.

One theme of particular importance that emerged was how the some-times subjective nature of apprehending risk can distort the public's per-ceptions of it. For example, three of our contributors referred to research on the biases occasioned by the availability of information. In essence, if lots of information is available, people may overestimate risk, and if only limited information is available then they may underestimate it. By this logic, making information available, and shedding light on a variety of risks, throughout the course of the lecture series may have led the audi-ence to overestimate the risks they faced from, for example, science in the media, terrorism, climate change or asteroid strikes.

Indeed, while publicising the lecture series on BBC Radio Cam-bridgeshire, the broadcaster who interviewed us had reached a similar conclusion. He asked whether, in holding a public lecture series on risk, we might 'scare' the audience. Of course, the answer to this question was resolutely no, not at all. We hoped that access to cutting-edge yet accessible research from eminent scholars and an opportunity to think deeply about risk would, in fact, empower people. It would recognise their agency and their capacity for confronting risk on their own terms, echoing Mary Beard's call that we should not be the 'victims' of risk, but active managers of it.

The lectures and essays also make clear, however, that this kind of empowerment involves not just management of the amount of information offered, but also a crucial degree of humility in the communication of risk. David Spiegelhalter's suggestion, that those in the public eye should acknowledge the uncertainties in the way we think about risk, resonated across all of the lectures. The existence of the 'unknown' and the 'unknown unknowns' is an important theme that ought to resonate further into the future, as should the idea that such uncertainties need to be acknowledged, not feared, by both the public and public officials.

These themes have many implications, not least on how public officials make and communicate decisions on our behalf. But what is clear is this; even the most mathematically minded of 'risk professionals' admit that 'risk intelligence' – the ability to make well-reasoned decisions about the risks we face – will never come solely from mathematical formula. The way forward will have to entail a much more complicated blend of mathematical, social, psychological, scientific, political and historical input – a blend that we feel this book has much to contribute to.

References

Beck, U. (1992) *Risk Society: Towards a New Modernity.* London: Sage.

Eidinow, E. (2007) *Oracles, Curses and Risk among the Ancient Greeks.* Oxford University Press.

Ericson, R. V. and Haggerty, R. V. (1997) *Policing the Risk Society.* Oxford University Press.

Farrington, D. P. (2007) 'Childhood risk factors and risk-focused prevention', in *The Oxford Handbook of Criminology*, ed. M. Maguire, R. Morgan and R. Reiner. Oxford University Press.

Feeley, M. and Simon, J. (1992) 'The new penology: notes on the emerging strategy of corrections and its implications', *Criminology* 30: 449–74.

Feeley, M. and Simon, J. (2003) 'The form and limits of the new penology', in *Punishment and Social Control*, ed. T. G. Blomberg and S. Cohen. New York: Aldine de Gruyter.

Gallant, T. (1991) *Risk and Survival in Ancient Greece.* Cambridge: Polity Press.

Gardner, D. (2008) *Risk: The Science and Politics of Fear*. London: Virgin Books.

Garnsey, P. (1988) *Famine and Food Supply in the Graeco-Roman World: Responses to Risk and Crisis*. Cambridge University Press.

Halstead, P. and O'Shea, J. (eds.) (1989) *Bad Year Economics: Cultural Responses to Risk and Uncertainty*. Cambridge University Press.

Mellor, D. H. (1988) 'Preface', in *The Darwin College Lectures: Origins*, ed. A. C. Fabian. Cambridge University Press.

2 Quantifying uncertainty

DAVID SPIEGELHALTER

Putting numbers on risks

Risk is a strange concept. Different disciplines have tried to define it precisely, but perhaps it is better to be informal and follow more popular usage. I shall take it as *anything to do with situations where 'bad' (or 'good') things may, or may not, happen.* The crucial elements are that there is uncertainty, and that the outcomes may be nice or nasty.

A wealth of recent psychological research has shown that we mainly use 'gut feelings' to deal with such situations, rather than carefully weighing up the consequences and assessing numerical probabilities, as more formal approaches would have us do. Our feelings are influenced by culture, our experiences and those of people close to us, media coverage, emotional feelings of dread, or hope, and so on, but we manage to get by most of the time, and it is noticeable how recently, in historical terms, the theory combining probability and 'rational' decision-making was developed. Even when evidence is available about the 'size' of a risk, in sufficiently stressful situations it may be ignored. Cass Sunstein, a senior adviser to Barack Obama, claims that people display 'probability neglect' when confronted with vivid images of terrorism, so that 'when their emotions are intensely engaged, people's attention is focused on the bad outcome itself, and they are inattentive to the fact that it is unlikely to occur'. So the 'true' risks are ignored; it's been shown that people are, rather illogically, willing to pay more for insurance against terrorism than insurance against all risks (which implicitly include terrorism), just because the use of the word conjures up dread.

But gut feelings might be unreliable in some circumstances, for example when people are trying to manipulate you to take some action, or when

David Spiegelhalter

the reasoning is complex and a lot depends on the decision. Then a more analytic, and perhaps rather unnatural, approach can be useful, whether you are an individual trying to make a personal decision, or you represent an organisation or government deciding on a policy in the face of uncertainty.

This more formal approach relies on putting numbers on probabilities of events, and raises the inevitable question: *can we quantify our uncertainty?* In this chapter we will just look at this question, ignoring our knowledge and feelings about the consequences of actions.

Putting probabilities on events

In some circumstances we can use pure logic to come up with reasonable probabilities, because of the assumed symmetries in the situation which allow equally likely outcomes to be specified. These are the classical areas of probability, with balanced coins, shuffled cards, and so on. For example, in the UK National Lottery six balls are drawn without replacement from a drum containing forty-nine numbered balls. If the numbers match the six numbers on your lottery ticket then you win, or share, the jackpot – fewer matches win less, with the lowest prize being ten pounds for three matching numbers.

If we assume that the lottery-drawing mechanism is completely fair and unbiased, so that each number is equally likely to be drawn, then we can immediately calculate the probabilities of specific events, such as a 1 in 13,983,815 chance of winning a jackpot, and a 1 in 56 chance of matching three numbers. Note the use of the word 'chance', deliberately carrying the connotation of an 'objective' number that can be calculated using the theory of probability.

If these probabilities are *assumed* to be known, because of the physical properties of the system, then we can learn nothing from history – even if the same lottery numbers came up every week we would have to put it down to luck. But even the slightest suspicion of irregularities changes everything, and suddenly the reassuring calculations evaporate if, for example, you suspect that some of the balls have been left out of the bag. The vital conclusion is that these 'classical' probabilities – chances that are states of the world – are grounded on

18

subjective assumptions about the generating mechanism, and hence are deeply contingent.

An alternative basis for quantifying uncertainty is by using historical data. If the future follows the same pattern as the past, then frequencies of events in history should reflect reasonable probabilities for events in the future. In fact the 'frequentist' view defines probability as the limiting frequency in a (fictitious) infinite replication. For example, sports betting companies use past data on football matches to propose reasonable odds for the results of future games. We have tried this, using fairly simple models involving estimates of the 'home advantage', 'attack strength' and 'defence weakness' of teams, that can be combined to give us expected numbers of goals in each match and hence, assuming a Poisson distribution around the expected values, a probability for any particular final score. Our own models have met with mixed success, but the (confidential) models used by professionals presumably work well enough to make money.

The assessed probabilities are therefore based on assumptions about the continuity of past with future, together with an assumed mathematical model for how various fictitious parameters such as 'attack strength' interact to give rise to appropriate odds. The lesson from this kind of exercise is that such assumptions are *known* to be false, or at least not precisely *true*, and yet the resulting probabilities may be good enough for the purpose. Again, the final numbers are contingent upon unprovable assumptions.

Finally, the situation may have neither reassuring symmetries nor useful historical precedents. For example, consider the situation in early 2008. The probability of Barack Obama becoming the next President of the United States could hardly be based on the empirical historical record of forty-three out of forty-three US Presidents being white. Philosophically, we might believe there is still some objective 'propensity' in the situation for Obama to be the next President, but this does not seem practically useful. Instead we are left to make a judgement using existing information, expressed as the betting odds that we are willing to place or to lay bets. These lead to the results shown in Figure 2.1, which are derived from a major online betting exchange. These 'probabilities' are not based on any 'objective' state of the world, nor historical data, and change

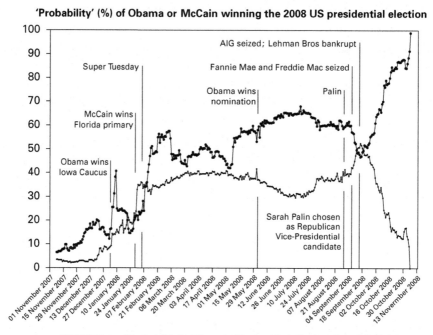

FIGURE 2.1 'Probability' of Barack Obama (dark line) or John McCain (light line) winning the 2008 US Presidential election, as reflected in the odds both taken and offered on a betting exchange, each day in the year up to the 2008 election.

constantly in receipt of further information. I would still argue that these are reasonable probabilities, as they reflect reasonable numerical uncertainty concerning the outcome, given the current state of knowledge.

These three circumstances – classical symmetry, historical data and subjective judgement – all lead to precisely the same conclusions. Probabilities are constructed on the basis of existing knowledge, and are therefore contingent. This rather dramatic conclusion, although open to dispute by some statisticians and philosophers of probability, has a respectable pedigree among the community of Bayesian statisticians. Indeed a guiding quote throughout my career comes from Bruno de Finetti:

Probability does not exist.

I take this to mean that probabilities are not states of the world (except possibly at the sub-atomic level, about which we are not concerned here), but depend on the relationship between the 'object' of the probability assessment, and the 'subject' who is doing the assessing. This means that, strictly speaking, we should not use the phrase '*the* probability *of* X', but '*my* probability *for* X', where 'my' refers to whoever is taking responsibility for the probability. This makes clear that probability expresses a relationship, not a property or an objective fact about X. Sadly, this phrasing is unlikely to become standard practice.

The second guiding quote for my career comes from a great industrial statistician, George Box:

> All models are wrong, but some are useful.

Again, this emphasises that the mathematical structures that we construct in order to arrive at numerical probabilities are not states of the world, but are based on unprovable assumptions. We shall look briefly at the deeper uncertainties concerned with model-building in a later section.

Representing probabilities

There is a wide range of alternatives for representing probabilities when communicating with different audiences. Here we discuss a limited list of options, and briefly summarise some of the psychological research related to the perception of the magnitudes of probabilities associated with the different representations.

By putting my personal information through a computer program, for example, my general practitioner can tell me that I have around a '10 per cent chance' of a heart attack or stroke in the next ten years. How might such a quantity be communicated to me? We first consider the use of text, either using words or numbers:

- **Natural language**: For example, 'you *might* have a heart attack or stroke', or 'it *is possible* you . . . '. Such language is widely used in weather forecasting. The interpretation of such terms is highly dependent on the subject: if numerical information is to be communicated, a fixed 'translation' might be agreed, such as in recent Intergovernmental Panel for Climate Change (IPCC) reports in which 'very likely' is taken to mean more than 90 per cent confidence in being correct.

- **Numerical probabilities defined between 0 and 1**: For example, 'Your probability of having a heart attack or stroke is 0.1.' This format is never used except in technical discussions.
- **Numerical 'chances' expressed as percentages**: 'You have a 10 per cent chance . . .'. This is widely used in popular discourse, but has connotations of random devices such as dice, which can appear inappropriate when discussing serious personal issues.
- **Numerical 'odds'**: 'You have a 1 in 10 chance of . . .'. This is a more popular expression, although it is still in terms of chances, but means that smaller probabilities are associated with larger numbers. Recent evidence suggests that around 25 per cent of the adult population cannot say which is the largest risk out of the options '1 in 10', '1 in 1000', '1 in 100'.
- **Frequencies in populations**: For example, 'Out of 100 people like you, 10 will have a heart attack . . .'. This is becoming a common text representation in leaflets and computer programs designed to explain risks to medical patients. However, it requires one to see oneself as part of a group of similar people – a 'reference class' – and this could conflict with a self-image of uniqueness and lead to a denial of the relevance of the statement.
- **Frequencies out of 'possible futures'**: 'Out of 100 ways things might turn out for you over the next 10 years, you would be expected to have a heart attack or stroke in 10 of them.' This is a novel representation intended to encourage the immediacy and ownership of the risk. Philosophically it is very shaky: it is an uneasy mixture between a probability, constructed on available knowledge, and a frequency interpretation, as a proportion of a population of possible futures.

There is also a range of graphical options, including pie charts, circles representing the size of the risk, bar charts, icon-plots showing many small 'people', 'Smilies' showing multiple iconic faces experiencing different outcomes, multiple photos, and word-clouds, in which the size of the font is proportional to the probability of the event.

None of these presents a universal solution. Challenges that arise include:

1. Comparing rare and more common events, leading to the frequent use of graphics on a logarithmic scale, or providing a 'magnifying glass' for zooming in on rarer events.
2. Graphical representation of multiple outcomes for the same individual.

3. Comparisons between alternative options when each brings a mixture of potential harms and benefits.
4. Uncertainty, in the sense that we may be more confident about some probabilities than others. While in principle this is of limited relevance, and may only add additional complexity, it could be an option for more sophisticated users.

All these formats deal with probabilities of single events, rather than uncertainty about continuous quantities such as future income, where a wide range of additional graphical tools would be necessary. Uncertainty about the time until an event, such as death, requires a representation for the distribution of possible survival times, for which there is a further range of options which are not explored here.

When it comes to evaluating different formats, it is important to be clear about the purpose of the representation. Broadly, we can divide the aims into:

- Gaining immediate attention and interest.
- Communicating information to be retained.
- Influencing continuing behaviour.

There are clear similarities between these objectives and those of commodity and service marketing. It would be intellectually satisfying to find that the three objectives follow a nice causal pathway: gaining interest leads to knowledge retention which influences behaviour. However, the research literature suggests that the relationship between these objectives is complex, if it exists at all. We must therefore be clear about what we are trying to achieve. For shared-care decisions in health, for example, we may want to provide information so that everyone feels they have made an informed choice, but without necessarily directly trying to influence behaviour in one direction or another. Research suggests that many people strongly welcome information provision, but then seek a fairly paternalistic form of advice ('I really appreciate you telling me all this, doctor, but what do you think I should do?')

There are possibilities for combining many of these representations within a single interface using interactive animations. Given that there is no single 'best' representation, this seems an appropriate policy so that users can essentially choose, or be guided towards, the format that they find most natural and comprehensible. And of course we must remember that people are likely to be much more influenced by their trust in the information source, their personal experiences and their feelings about the possible outcomes, than they are by the particular choice of format. Nevertheless, it seems a reasonable duty to try and do our best to make sure that the available evidence is permitted to play a role in personal decisions.

Communicating small lethal risks

There are particular problems in comparing and communicating small lethal risks, and yet this is what many of us are faced with in our daily lives. Ideally we need a 'friendly' unit of deadly risk. A suggestion made in the 1970s by Ronald Howard is the use of the *micromort*, or a one-in-a-million chance of death. This is attractive as it generally means that we can translate small risks into whole numbers that can be immediately compared. For example, the risk of death from a general anaesthetic (not the accompanying operation), is quoted as 1 in 100,000, meaning that in every 100,000 operations we would expect one death. This corresponds to ten micromorts per operation.

We can also consider the 18,000 people out of 54 million in England and Wales who died from non-natural causes in 2008, such as accidents, murders, suicides, and so on. This corresponds to an average of $18,000 / (54 \times 365) \approx 1$ micromort per day, so we can think of a micromort as the average 'ration' of lethal risk that people spend each day, and which we do not unduly worry about. A one-in-a-million chance of death can also be thought of as the consequences of a bizarre game in which twenty coins are thrown in the air, and if they all come down heads the thrower has to commit suicide. It is interesting to explore, in a fictitious context, the amount people would accept as payment to take part in the game.

A measure such as a micromort needs a unit of exposure to accompany it, and different sources of risk naturally give rise to different levels of exposure. Here we briefly consider transport, medical events, and leisure activities. Of course, we can only quote 'average' risks over a population, which neither represent 'your' risks nor necessarily those of a random person drawn from the population. Nevertheless they provide useful 'ballpark' figures from which reasonable odds for specific situations might

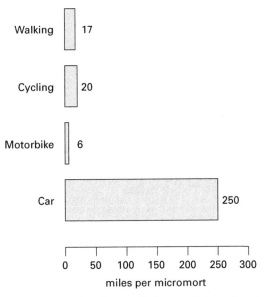

FIGURE 2.2 Distance travelled per micromort (one-in-a-million chance of death) for different forms of transport in the UK, based on assumption of constant risk within transport type and over time.

be assessed. As we have already emphasised, we do not consider that numerical risks exist as fully estimable properties of the world.

Transport

Options for comparing forms of transport include miles per micromort, micromort per 100 miles, micromorts per hour, and so on. We compare the first two options below. Although the general advice is that larger numbers should correspond to larger risks, 'miles per micromort' seems attractive, especially when used to provide a 'calibration' against other risks.

We have not included trains and planes as they would require a change in axes, and the rarity of fatalities (even though they are given great coverage) makes assessment of 'average' risk of limited value.

Medical events

Since these are specific, discrete occurrences, the natural measure is risk per event, for example giving birth, having a Caesarean section or having a general anaesthetic. The exception is spending time in hospital, which

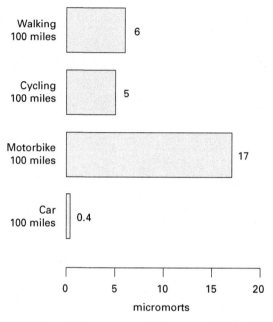

FIGURE 2.3 Micromorts per distance travelled for different forms of transport in the UK, based on assumption of constant risk within transport type and over time.

is expressed as micromorts per night spent in hospital, considering only deaths that were not due to natural causes.

Examination of Figures 2.2 and 2.4 is informative. For example, having a general anaesthetic carries the same risk of death, on average, as travelling 60 miles on a motorbike. The high value for a night in hospital is derived from the National Patient Safety Agency reports of adverse events resulting in death. If anything, this is an underestimate.

Leisure activities

We assume that the risk comes from a specific 'accident' in what is an otherwise safe activity with no chronic ill effects. It is therefore natural to express exposure as the specific activity. Since the activities take different lengths of time it would be possible to express them as micromorts per hour, but this does not seem to reflect the choices that people make.

All these examples concern sudden deaths, but many 'risky' behaviours have a delayed impact, such as smoking or an unhealthy diet. Comparing

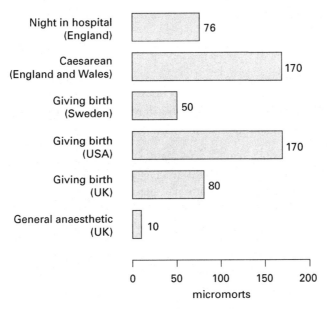

FIGURE 2.4 Micromorts per medical event in 2008, based on assumption of constant risk within event type and over time.

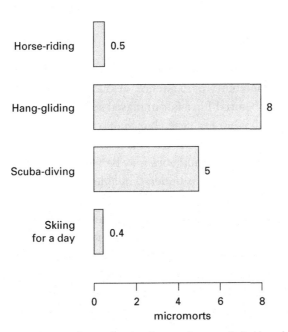

FIGURE 2.5 Approximate micromorts per activity, based on assumption of constant risk within activity and over time.

'acute' and 'chronic' risks is tricky, but there have been a number of suggestions for 'riskometers' which attempt to put both immediate and delayed risks on a common scale. Options include:

1. Listing causes of death, which allows a comparison of how many people, for example, die from accidents compared to heart disease, but does not directly allow the comparison of alternative daily activities.
2. Transform lifetime risks, say of dying from cancer due to smoking, into risk per day by assuming that there are, say, around 30,000 days in a lifetime. But no allowance is made for delayed effects.
3. Discount future risks by a specified factor, and assess the proportional loss on discounted life-expectancy due to different activities. This can then be converted to a logarithmic scale.

None of these options seems entirely satisfactory, as they inevitably mean placing, for example, cigarette smoking and motorcycle riding on a common risk scale, and yet these two behaviours have very different consequences.

Epistemic uncertainty

We have seen how the theory of probability is used as a tool in analysing the essential unpredictability of existence, also known as *aleatory* uncertainty. For example, before I flip a fair unbiased coin, people are generally willing to say there is a 50 per cent chance of a head. However, if I flip the coin and then cover up the result, and ask what is the probability of a head, after some grumbling an audience may be willing to admit the odds are still 50:50. Their misgiving is understandable – they need to cross an important line in being willing to use numerical probabilities to express their *epistemic* uncertainty, that is, their ignorance about what the coin actually shows. What then if I look at the coin and ask them the for probability of a head? After an even longer pause they may grudgingly admit it is still 50:50. Now they have been dragged into the full recognition that epistemic uncertainty is not a property of the object, in this case the coin; it is a property of their relationship with the object, and we all may have different epistemic uncertainties depending on the knowledge to which we are privy. This is the essence of the Bayesian approach to statistics. It allows us to use probability theory to express epistemic uncertainty.

Table 2.1 *Scoring procedure when expressing your confidence as a probability of being correct*

Your 'probability' that your answer is correct (out of 10)	5	6	7	8	9	10
Score if you are **right**	0	9	16	21	24	25
Score if you are *wrong*	0	−11	−24	−39	−56	−75

Of course a problem arises when we are deluded about the knowledge we have and claim certainty, or at least high confidence, in facts that are not actually the case. Fortunately there is an under-appreciated branch of statistics concerned with assessing the quality of people's probability judgements using what are known as scoring rules. These are designed to penalise people for providing poor probabilities for events whose truth or falsity is later determined.

We can illustrate the issues with some simple questions given below. In each case either (A) or (B) is the correct answer, and the challenge is to decide which answer you feel is most likely to be correct, and quantify your probability that your answer is correct. So if you are certain (A) is correct then you should give it 10/10, but if you are only around 70 per cent sure then it gets 7/10. If you have no idea, then give 5/10 to either choice.

1. Which is higher: (A) the Eiffel tower, or (B) Canary Wharf?
2. Who is older: (A) George Osborne, or (B) Nick Clegg?
3. In the International Movie DataBase rankings (29/12/2009), which film comes higher: (A) *The Matrix*, or (B) *Forrest Gump*?
4. Which is bigger: (A) Croatia, or (B) Czech Republic?
5. Which is bigger: (A) Venus, or (B) Earth?
6. Who died first: (A) Beethoven, or (B) Napoleon?

Table 2.1 shows how you are scored when the true answer is revealed. If you are absolutely correct then you score twenty-five, but if completely wrong then you lose seventy-five. If your probability was five for either answer, then you stay where you were. It is clear that there is a steep penalty for being confident and wrong. This is not arbitrary punishment, but a consequence of designing a scoring rule that encourages honesty, so that if you are 70 per cent sure of, say (A), then your expected score is maximised if you give a probability of 7/10 for (A), rather than exaggerating and giving a probability of 10/10 for (A). Such a scoring rule is called 'proper'.

By subtracting twenty-five from each of the scores it becomes clear that the penalty is dependent on the square of the probability given to the wrong answer. This quadratic, or Brier, scoring rule was developed to train weather forecasters to give reasonable probability of future weather events such as rain. A simple linear scoring rule, such as scoring somebody by the probability given to the correct answer, is inappropriate as it would encourage people to exaggerate their confidence in being right.

This process shows that epistemic uncertainties can be quantified as probabilities, which are necessarily subjective and expressed by an individual on the basis of available knowledge. They should not be thought of as embodying some 'true belief', but are *constructed* by whatever elicitation process is being used. But for these judgements to be useful, people's probabilities need to have some reasonable properties. First, they should be *calibrated*, in the sense that if someone gives a probability of 7/10 to a series of events, then, around 70 per cent of those events should actually occur. Second, the probabilities should *discriminate*, in that events that occur should be given higher probabilities than those that do not. It can be shown that a proper scoring rule rewards both calibration and discrimination.

So far we have considered events that are well defined and whose truth can be established. In real situations things are generally not so simple, as we shall explore in the next section.

Deeper uncertainties

In 1921 Frank Knight published his book *Risk, Uncertainty and Profit,* in which he distinguished between 'risk' and 'uncertainty'. 'Risks' were objective quantities that could either be obtained by reasoning (for example, symmetric situations involving dice, cards, etc.), or estimated from historical data. Conversely, 'uncertainty' was subjective and judgemental, and not susceptible to objective measurement. Since that time the use of subjective probabilities has become developed and so, as our discussion in earlier sections shows, it may be considered reasonable to use numbers to express our subjective beliefs. However, there will still be many circumstances in which we feel that our ignorance is so great, or the future possibilities so ill-defined, that we are unwilling to express numerical judgements with any confidence.

We may also have the courage and insight to acknowledge that there may be important things we have not even thought of like the Rumsfeldian 'unknown unknowns'. A famous plea for such humility came from Oliver Cromwell. In 1650 he was trying to avoid a battle with the Church of Scotland, which was then supporting the return of Charles I's son. He wrote: 'Is it therefore infallibly agreeable to the Word of God, all that *you* say? I beseech you, in the bowels of Christ, think it possible you may be mistaken.'

If we are willing to entertain the possibility that we may be mistaken, then it may mean we have crossed the border of quantifiable uncertainty, and opened up the possibility of non-numerical expressions of our doubts and ignorance after we have constructed a model from which we want to derive risk assessments. These misgivings may take many forms. For example, we might conduct analyses under alternative sets of assumptions, and examine the robustness of our conclusions. We may admit to aspects of the world that we know have not been adequately included, and informally express our judgement as to their importance. We may express judgements as to the strength and quality of the evidence underlying our model and so express limits to our confidence in some conclusions. We may add on a 'fudge factor' to allow for all the things we may not have thought of. Finally, we may, of course, choose to deny non-modelled uncertainty, or unwittingly overlook errors in our model. One can see examples of these strategies being played out in the deliberations about climate change.

Conclusions

We have shown how our uncertainties about events can be quantified using probability theory, whether or not there is a firm logical or historical basis for these assessments. By taking a Bayesian perspective, we can extend the use of probability to cover our epistemic uncertainties about well-defined quantities. We may even, in some circumstances, quantify our uncertainty about the appropriate model to use. But when we start acknowledging our inability to represent the full complexity of the real world using mathematical models, we are faced with leaving the safe land of quantifiable uncertainty and entering the (possibly hostile) environment of disputed science, ill-understood possibilities and deep uncertainty.

This is a world in which many statisticians and mathematical scientists feel very uncomfortable, and for which they receive no training. A good start to their education might involve acknowledging that their models are inadequate constructs derived from currently accepted knowledge, and that numerical probabilities are not a property of the world but an expression of their subjective understanding of the world. These may be considered fairly radical ideas.

On the other hand, those tasked with taking action on the basis of risk assessments derived from a formal model also need to accept their provisional and contingent nature, and the associated deep uncertainties. This they may be reluctant to do, in their desire for concrete guides on which they can base decisions.

My own feeling is that, when decision-makers are dealing with 'expert' risk assessments based on models, there should be quantification of uncertainty to the maximum possible extent. But the potential limitations of these numerical assessments should be acknowledged. A language is also required for communicating, with due humility and without fear of casual rejection, the deeper uncertainties.

Answers to quiz

A, B, A, B, B, B

Acknowledgements

I would like to thank Mike Pearson and Ian Short with help in preparing animations and illustrations for the lecture, Ted Harding for constructing Figure 2.1, and Frank Duckworth for discussions on micromorts and riskometers.

References

Box, G. (1979) *Robustness in Statistics: Proceedings of a Workshop*. New York: Academic Press.

De Finetti, B. (1974) *Theory of Probability: A Critical Introductory Treatment*. London, New York: Wiley.

Galesic, M. and Garcia-Retamero, R. (2010) 'Statistical numeracy for health: a cross-cultural comparison with probabilistic national samples', *Archives of Internal Medicine* 170 (5): 462–8.

Gigerenzer, G. (2010) *Rationality for Mortals: How People Cope with Uncertainty*. New York: Oxford University Press.

Knight, F. (1921) *Risk, Uncertainty and Profit*. Available at: www.econlib.org/library/Knight/knRUP.html.

Lindley, D. (2006) *Understanding Uncertainty*. Hoboken, NJ: Wiley.

Lipkus, I. M. (2007) 'Numeric, verbal, and visual formats of conveying health risks: suggested best practices and future recommendations', *Medical Decision Making* 27 (5): 696–713.

Micromort – Wikipedia, the free encyclopedia. Available at: en.wikipedia.org/wiki/Micromort (accessed 23 August 2010).

Morgan, G., Dowlatabadi, H., Henrion, M. et al. 'Best practice approaches for characterizing, communicating, and incorporating scientific uncertainty in decision making'. Final Report, CCSP Synthesis and Assessment Product 5–2. Available at: www.climatescience.gov/Library/sap/sap5–2/final-report/default.htm (accessed 10 July 2010).

Sunstein, C. R. (2003) 'Terrorism and probability neglect', *Journal of Risk and Uncertainty* 26: 121–36.

3 Decisions, risk and the brain

JOHN P. O'DOHERTY

Introduction

The ability to make good decisions about future courses of action under conditions of uncertainty is essential for the survival of most animals, including humans. Whether it is deciding which item to choose from a restaurant menu, when to cross a busy road or what career path to follow, we are constantly faced with the need to make decisions of varying degrees of importance in terms of their implications for our future well-being. Often the outcomes of such decisions are highly uncertain, and we must therefore take into account not only the pros and cons of the outcomes associated with different courses of action but also the uncertainties or 'risk' attached to such outcomes. On the whole, humans are rather good at making decisions, as exemplified by our incredible success as a species. The root of that success necessarily lies in the machinery contained in our brain, a highly efficient computer weighing approximately 1.36 kg that has been shaped by evolution to allow us the flexibility to make good decisions in diverse and rapidly changing environments. In this chapter, I will give a broad introduction to a new interdisciplinary field of study called 'neuroeconomics', which is concerned with elucidating how the brain is capable of enabling us to make such good decisions. I will outline our current understanding about how decisions are made by the brain, and I will highlight some of the outstanding questions for future research in this still nascent field of study.

Neuroeconomics

The field of neuroeconomics has emerged through a fusion of approaches found in more traditional disciplines. These include not only neuroscience and economics, as one might have guessed from the perhaps clumsily put-together title, but also cognitive and behavioural psychology, computer science and artificial intelligence, engineering, robotics and behavioural ecology, among others (Glimcher et al., 2009). A core assumption behind neuroeconomics is (in common with much if not all contemporary neuroscience) that the brain can be treated as a computational device transforming input in the form of information reaching our sense organs (vision, touch, audition, smell and taste), into output in the form of the generation of behaviour. This transformation is mediated by the billions of highly interconnected neurons (nerve cells) contained in our brains. The main goal of neuroscience is to describe precisely how these neurons act on the incoming sensory information in order to produce a particular output, or, to return to the brain-as-computer analogy, to resolve the algorithms (or mathematical functions) used by the brain to achieve such transformations.

Neuroeconomics takes as its starting point the assumption that people (or, to be more specific, their brains) use particular algorithms to enable them to make decisions, and that ultimately it will be possible to describe such algorithms using precise mathematical formalisms. Another core assumption is that the only way to gain a precise understanding of how such algorithms work is by looking inside the brain and actively mapping the neural circuits underlying the decision process. In other words, it is not sufficient merely to observe the behaviour of people as they make decisions (as psychologists and behavioural economists have done in the past), but rather it is necessary also to understand the wiring in the brain that gives rise to such behaviour.

Before peering into the brain, I will first review some basic concepts relevant for human decision-making from two of the traditional fields on which neuroeconomics has been built: economics and psychology.

Utility in economics

A pervasive idea in economics is the notion of utility (Bernoulli, 1954). In the words of the nineteenth-century utilitarian philosopher Jeremy Bentham, utility can be conceived of as:

John P. O'Doherty

> any property in an object whereby it tends to produce benefit, advantage,
> pleasure, good or happiness ... or ... to prevent the happening of
> mischief, pain, evil or unhappiness.
>
> (Bentham, 1987: 66)

The fundamental assumption underlying neoclassical economics is that a rational individual will always choose to take those actions yielding the maximum possible future utility out of a selection of possible actions – that is, when faced with the choice of apples versus oranges, if choosing apples has a higher utility than oranges, then I will choose apples. Utility also has a subjective property, in that while I may find apples to have a higher utility than oranges, someone else may rank oranges higher than apples. Traditional economists do not need to assume consistency of utility judgements across individuals, but rather do assume that individuals are internally consistent in their application of utility to express preferences: if I prefer apples to oranges, and also prefer oranges to lemons, then it follows that if given a choice between apples and lemons I should also prefer apples to lemons. Based on the axiomatic assumption that people are rational and internally consistent in their use of utility to guide choice, neoclassical economists have built up very sophisticated and elegant mathematical frameworks to describe how economic systems should function in principle, starting with choices made by single individuals, extending to competitive interactions between individuals, and scaling up to the behaviour of markets, trading systems and countries (Von Neumann and Morgenstern, 1944).

While this approach has been hugely influential and given rise to a vast array of invaluable mathematical tools for studying choice, such as game theory, some cracks began to appear in this framework almost as soon as it was formalised. The trouble was that, though the framework was logically coherent and mathematically elegant, the core assumption that people are always 'rational' and internally consistent in their allocation of choices was found to be not always true (Allais, 1953; Kahneman and Tversky, 1984), thereby challenging the extent to which the framework was actually useful in understanding real choice behaviour. This finding at least in part has given the impetus for some economists to focus not on how choices should be made in principle, but rather on the empirical study of how people actually make choices in the real world (Smith, 1982), which then led to consideration of how such choices are computed directly in the brain, and ultimately the field of neuroeconomics. Although neuroeconomists may have abandoned the assumption that people are *always* rational or consistent in their choices, the notion that choices are taken for the purpose of maximising expected or anticipated utility remains a central assumption. However, neuroeconomists also recognise that the ability to compute utilities and use those computations in different circumstances depends on the underlying neural circuitry, the structure of which may sometimes impose constraints or bounds on the extent to which choice will be fully consistent and rational. As we shall see, a major focus of contemporary neuroeconomics is to try to understand how utilities are represented in the brain, as well as to gain insight into the constraints imposed by such neural circuits, leading to violations of the assumptions of rational expected utility theory as formalised by the economists.

Reinforcers and psychology

A set of concepts related to utility has been developed in psychology, particularly the branch of psychology concerned with studying how animals learn from experience. Observation of the behaviour of any animal reveals that animals can increase or decrease the rate at which they perform particular behaviours depending on the outcome of those behaviours. A positive reinforcer is any outcome that results in an increase in the rate or probability of any behaviour on which such an outcome depends, whereas a negative reinforcer is any outcome that results in a decrease in the rate of probability of a behaviour. A reinforcer is defined as anything that changes the probability of an animal's behaviour, and the inference can be made that a given stimulus is a reinforcer through observation of the animal's behaviour in the presence of that stimulus; an economist might similarly infer a given object has utility by observing the preferences made by an individual.

Many different objects or stimuli in the world can act as reinforcers for animals, including humans. Some reinforcers are thought to be primary or basic, in that they are composed of biologically relevant substances required for survival or procreation and are presumed to have 'innate' or unlearned value. Other 'secondary' reinforcers are proposed not to have 'innate' or primary reinforcer value, but rather to have acquired such value through being associated over the course of experience with more primary reinforcers. Often cited examples of positive primary reinforcers are carbohydrates (such as sugars) and water, whereas a canonical example of a secondary reinforcer in human society is money, which has no intrinsic value but rather has acquired value through being associated with the procurement of other more basic reinforcers such as food, water, shelter, etc. Actually, establishing which reinforcers are primary in the sense that they have truly 'innate' unlearned value is a challenging area of research in its own right (de Araujo et al., 2008; Steiner et al., 2001). Almost certainly complex foods are not primary reinforcers but rather have acquired value through learning or through integration of more basic constituent reinforcers. Possible candidates for primary reinforcers are sweet, salty and bitter tastes, the smell of rotten food (which indicates the likely presence of harmful bacteria or toxins), pain (signalling tissue damage) or even the detection of internal changes in blood glucose levels that follow from consuming foods (de Araujo et al., 2008). As must now be apparent, the concept of a reinforcer from psychology appears to have a lot in common with that of the concept of utility from economics – a positive reinforcer is something that would increase an individual's overall utility, whereas a negative reinforcer would decrease overall utility.

The important contributions of animal-learning psychology to neuro-economics goes far beyond the concept of reinforcement. Animal learning is concerned with understanding the principles underlying the ability of animals to learn from experience and produce behaviour based on previously acquired associations. Most of the decisions we make in the course of our everyday lives are made in the absence of complete information about the outcome of such decisions. For instance, when choosing an item on a restaurant menu we don't know exactly what the food will taste like when it arrives. Instead, we have to rely on our past learning and experience: maybe we have tasted that item before in the same or a different restaurant, maybe we are able to take advantage of other information from the environment about what kind of food is likely to be served, information such as whether the restaurant has plastic chairs and laminate walls or fine mahogany furnishings and silk wallpaper. There-fore, as will become apparent later, ideas from animal-learning psychology about how animals can learn from experience have proved to be indis-pensable in trying to gain a handle on how particular parts of the brain implement learning from experience and facilitate the use of such learned information in guiding decisions.

Cognitive neurology of decision-making: the case of Phineas Gage and beyond

Now that some basic concepts from economics and psychology have been outlined, we can begin to explore how decisions are mediated by the brain. We will start with the localisation of decision-making to particular brain structures. Perhaps the first reported localisation of decision-making to a particular part of the brain arose from the now famous case of Phineas Gage (Harlow, 1848). Gage was a railroad construction worker whose job consisted of blasting rock to clear a path for the railroad. To achieve this he would drill a hole in the rock which would subsequently be filled with 'blasting powder'. This was then covered with sand and compacted using a tamping iron. The powder was then detonated, once the workers had withdrawn to a safe distance, in order to blast apart the surrounding rock. On 13 September 1848 outside the town of Cavendish, Vermont, Gage was in the process of compacting a blast-powder-filled hole using the tamping iron when it exploded (possibly because the sand had been omitted). Unfortunately for Gage, the tamping iron was propelled with force by the explosion through the air and penetrated his skull through his left eyeball; it carried on through his brain, where it broke through the skull on the top of his head. The brain tissue in the path of the tamping iron would have been completely destroyed. Remarkably, Gage survived the injury and was returned to health under the care of the physician J. M. Harlow. In the months following the injury Harlow reported a number of changes in Gage's personality and behaviour as described by his friends and colleagues:

> The equilibrium or balance, so to speak, between his intellectual faculties and animal propensities, seems to have been destroyed. He is fitful,

irreverent, indulging at times in the grossest profanity (which was not previously his custom), manifesting but little deference for his fellows, impatient of restraint or advice when it conflicts with his desires, at times pertinaciously obstinate, yet capricious and vacillating, devising many plans of future operations, which are no sooner arranged than they are abandoned in turn for others appearing more feasible...

(1868: 339-40)

From this description it seems that at least two psychological changes have occurred in Gage (if we are to take Harlow's rather anecdotal report at face value): first of all, his personality appears to have changed so that he has become impulsive, risk-taking, socially inappropriate and insensitive to the feelings of others. Secondly, Gage appears to be exhibiting difficulties in making decisions: he is 'capricious and vacillating', making many plans for future action which he suddenly abandons in pursuit of alternative actions.

Over a hundred years later, computer-based reconstruction of the likely path of the tamping iron through Gage's skull by Hanna Damasio and colleagues at the University of Iowa (Damasio et al., 1994) revealed that the area of the brain likely to have been most damaged by the injury is a region called the ventromedial prefrontal cortex (vmPFC; Figure 3.1A). This area is a part of the frontal lobes, and is located approximately behind the forehead, above the orbits of the eyes (eye sockets), extending further up underneath the middle part of the forehead, from the gap between the eyebrows up to the top of the forehead (Figure 3.1B). In order to study the effects of damage to this area on decision-making in a more methodical manner Antoine Bechara and colleagues, also at the University of Iowa, recruited a group of patients who had sustained damage to this region from a variety of causes, such as the removal by surgery of tissue affected by a tumorous growth in this area, or damage to this area following a stroke (Figure 3.1C) (Bechara, Damasio and Damasio, 2000). They tested these patients in the laboratory on a simple decision-making task that has since become known as the Iowa Gambling Task. The task presents patients with a choice between four different 'decks of cards' (Figure 3.1D). On each trial the patient must select a card from one of the decks in order to try to win money. Depending on the choice they make, they are subsequently informed that they have won some money,

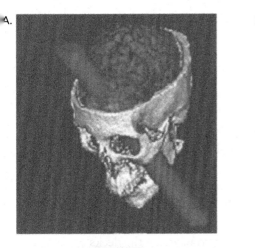

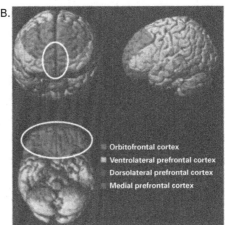

Orbitofrontal cortex
Ventrolateral prefrontal cortex
Dorsolateral prefrontal cortex
Medial prefrontal cortex

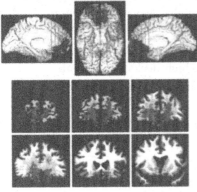

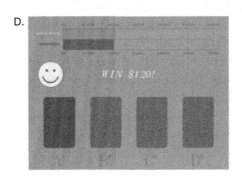

WIN $120!

FIGURE 3.1 **A**: Computer-generated reconstruction of the path of the tamping iron through the skull of Phineas Gage, showing path of the iron through the ventromedial prefrontal cortex.
B: Illustration of the main anatomical constituent parts of the prefrontal cortex. The ventromedial prefrontal cortex spans the area indicated by the white ellipses, including the lower part of the medial prefrontal cortex (top left, circled), and the orbitofrontal cortex on the underside of the frontal lobes (bottom left, circled). The three images show the brain from different perspectives: the top left shows the front of the brain as if looking head on, the top right shows the brain from a side view, and the bottom left shows the brain from the underside.
C: Image showing damage to parts of the ventromedial prefrontal cortex in a group of 13 patients who were tested for decision-making deficits on the Iowa Gambling Task by Bechara and colleagues. The darkened area of brain tissue shows the region of vmPFC exhibiting damage in at least 4 patients.
D: Illustration of the computerised version of the Iowa gambling task. Patients on each trial choose a card from one of four decks. Depending on the card chosen they receive feedback depicting an amount of imaginary money won (shown here is a trial where $120 has been won). On some trials subjects also lose money. Different decks yield differing amounts of cumulative gains and losses, with two decks yielding more gains on average than losses (advantageous decks), while the other two decks yield more losses than gains on average (disadvantageous). In order to win as much money as possible patients must learn to choose from the advantageous decks and avoid the disadvantageous ones. Patients with damage to ventromedial prefrontal cortex have major difficulties in performing this task.

the amounts varying, and sometimes they are told that they have lost money, again the amounts varying. Two of the decks are set up (unbeknownst to the patients) to be disadvantageous, in that, if those decks are chosen repeatedly, the patient will end up losing, cumulatively, more money than they win, whereas the other two decks are advantageous in that those decks will, if chosen, lead to cumulatively more money being gained than is lost. The task is inherently difficult to solve, in that it is not immediately obvious either to a patient with vmPFC damage or a neurologically healthy person with an intact brain which of the decks are advantageous or disadvantageous. Instead, this must be learned through trial and error by repeatedly sampling from the different decks. While healthy volunteers or patients with damage to some other parts of the brain can succeed in eventually working out which decks are advantageous and which are not, and therefore start to favour choosing from the advantageous decks, patients with damage to the vmPFC were found to have considerable difficulties in performing the task. By the end of the task, a typical vmPFC patient was much more likely to continue choosing from the disadvantageous decks than a healthy control subject. Bechara et al. therefore showed in a controlled and systematic way in the neuropsychological laboratory that damage to this region appears to be critical for at least some kinds of decision-making. Although there is still much debate about the nature of the decision-making impairment following damage to the vmPFC, the finding that vmPFC is important for decision-making has been replicated many times subsequently, using different types of tasks and in patients with different types of neurological injury or disease impacting on this region. Now that we have established that this area appears to be necessary for decision-making, the next question that can be asked is, precisely what computations or algorithms are being implemented in this region to underlie this capacity?

Decision utility, experienced utility and the brain

Returning to ideas we reviewed earlier, recall that a fundamental notion in economics is that the goal of a rational decision-making agent is to choose those actions which maximise that agent's expected utility. It follows that in order to understand how the brain is capable of making decisions, the first thing we might want to do is look into the brain and try to determine whether utility is indeed represented in the brain through patterns of neural activity and, if so, where such representations are located. Before exploring how to go about doing this, it is worthwhile making a distinction between two different types of utility: decision and experienced utility (Kahneman, Wakker and Sarin, 1997). Decision utility represents a computation about the expected future utility that is predicted to follow from choosing a particular action. Different available actions will have different decision utilities assigned to them, and it is by comparing the decision utilities (to find the best one) that decisions are ultimately taken. Experienced utility, by contrast, represents the valuation response that occurs when an outcome is actually experienced, that is when the meal ordered at the restaurant is finally consumed, or when money is won or lost after playing a slot machine. Experienced utility is an evaluation of the hedonic properties of an outcome – that is, how or good or bad this makes me feel. Before turning to the brain mechanisms of decision utility, let us first consider how experienced utility is represented neurally.

Neural representation of experienced utility

How can one study the representation of experienced utility in the brain? Well, perhaps the simplest thing one could do is give different stimuli to people, allow them to experience or consume them, ask them to report how pleasant they find the items as they are consuming them, while at the same time measuring neural activity and testing for activity patterns that happen to correlate or co-vary with the reported pleasantness.

To measure neural activity in the living brain in people, a range of different tools is now available. Arguably, the most powerful and certainly the most widely used of these techniques available at the present time is functional magnetic resonance imaging (fMRI). The dominant fMRI technique, BOLD (blood oxygenation level dependent), works by detecting changes in magnetic signals that occur due to changes in the proportion of oxygenated and deoxygenated blood in blood vessels close to neural activity. During periods of increased neural activity in a region, greater demands are made on blood vessels to increase the amounts of fresh oxygenated blood delivered to the vicinity of the neural activity in order to

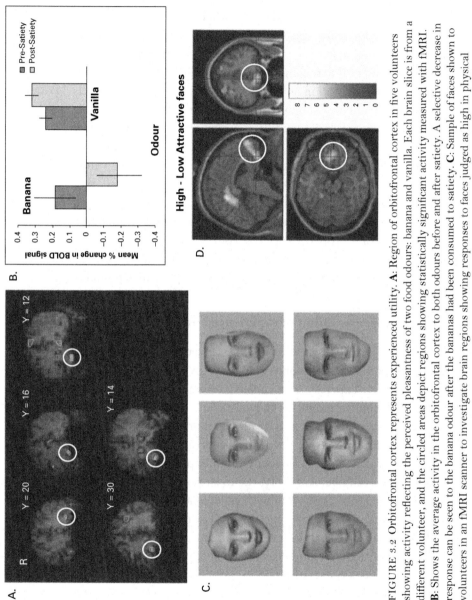

FIGURE 3.2 Orbitofrontal cortex represents experienced utility. **A**: Region of orbitofrontal cortex in five volunteers showing activity reflecting the perceived pleasantness of two food odours: banana and vanilla. Each brain slice is from a different volunteer, and the circled areas depict regions showing statistically significant activity measured with fMRI. **B**: Shows the average activity in the orbitofrontal cortex to both odours before and after satiety. A selective decrease in response can be seen to the banana odour after the bananas had been consumed to satiety. **C**: Sample of faces shown to volunteers in an fMRI scanner to investigate brain regions showing responses to faces judged as high in physical attractiveness compared to those judged as low in attractiveness. The faces shown here are drawn from the high-attractiveness set. **D**: Region of medial orbitofrontal cortex extending up to medial prefrontal cortex (circled) showing increased responses following presentation of high– compared to low–attractiveness faces. The three images show the same activated brain area from different perspectives.

increase quantities of oxygen and other nutrients available for sustaining the cellular processes underlying neural activity. Such a localised increase in blood oxygenation can be measured using fMRI because oxygenated and deoxygenated blood have different levels of magnetic susceptibility and hence give off different signals when measured in an MRI machine (for details of this method the reader is referred to Huettel, Song and McCarthy, 2004).

Returning to the question of experienced utility, a number of fMRI studies have been conducted on the question of where such utility is represented in the brain for a variety of types of reinforcers. O'Doherty and colleagues scanned the brains of hungry human volunteers while they were presented repeatedly with one of two different pleasant food odours, vanilla and banana (O'Doherty et al., 2000). Activity to the two odours was recorded with fMRI, and the subjects were then removed from the scanner and fed until they were satiated with bananas. This feeding process had the effect of decreasing the perceived pleasantness (or experienced utility) of the banana (because the associated food had been eaten to satiety), while leaving the pleasantness of the odour of the vanilla (corresponding to a food that was not eaten) unchanged (and still pleasant), a phenomenon called sensory-specific satiety. The subjects were then placed back in the scanner and activity was measured while they were being presented again with the two food odours. We then tested for brain regions showing a difference in response to the banana odours from pre- to post-satiety but that also showed no change to the vanilla odours. Any region exhibiting such a pattern was a candidate area for encoding of the subjective pleasantness of an odour. One region in the brain was found to show this pattern consistently across the volunteers: the orbitofrontal cortex, which is a constituent part of the ventromedial prefrontal cortex. Brain activity in this region was high in response to the presentation of the vanilla and banana odours during the first scan, when subjects found both odours to be pleasant. But during the second scan, activity was selectively decreased to the banana odour but not to the vanilla odour – that by contrast continued to show a strong positive response. This pattern of activity mirrored changes in the volunteer's perceived pleasantness for the odours, suggesting that the pleasantness or experienced utility of the odours was represented in this region (Fig. 3.2A, B).

Evidence of a role for the orbitofrontal cortex in representing experienced utility for stimuli in the visual domain was obtained by O'Doherty et al. (2003). In this experiment, volunteers were presented with pictures of different unfamiliar faces of varying levels of physical attractiveness and of both genders (Figure 3.2C). Brain activity in response to faces rated as being high in attractiveness was then compared to activity in response to faces rated as being low in attractiveness. A region of the orbitofrontal cortex was found to show very strong responses to faces ranked as being high in attractiveness compared to those faces ranked as being low in attractiveness, suggesting that the aesthetic judgment of attractiveness is represented in the orbitofrontal cortex (Figure 3.2D). Similar results have been obtained for monetary reward – brain activity in a similar part of the orbitofrontal cortex is correlated with the amount of money that an individual wins on a given trial while they play simple decision-making tasks (O'Doherty et al., 2001; Knutson et al., 2001; Elliott et al., 2003). A role for the orbitofrontal cortex in representing experienced utility has also been established for a wide variety of other types of stimuli including tastes, water, musical tones and even wine (Blood et al., 1999; de Araujo et al., 2003; Grabenhorst and Rolls, 2008; Plassmann et al., 2008). Collectively, these findings suggest a very general role for the orbitofrontal cortex in representing experienced utility.

From experienced to decision utility: learning and prediction errors

Now that we have evidence of a role for a part of the brain in representing experienced utility, we can turn our attention to decision utility – which, you will recall, corresponds to an expectation about the future experienced utility that follows from choosing a particular option. Before delving into where in the brain decision utilities are represented, let us consider how it might be possible to acquire utilities for different options in the world in the first place. As alluded to previously, most of the time we often cannot know from merely surveying the situation in the moment, how good or bad the choice of a particular option is going to be. Rather, we often have to rely on our experience about how things turned out when we were faced with similar decisions in the past, in order to have any clue about how best to respond in the present. A very influential idea, going back to the earliest days of animal-learning psychology at the beginning of the twentieth century, is that the ability to use past experience to guide future choice arises from trial and error learning, that is by repeatedly taking particular actions and then observing the outcomes of those actions (Thorndike, 1898). The experienced utility of those outcomes is then used to modulate the probability of taking those actions again in future: actions leading to an increase in experienced utility should be performed more often in future, whereas those leading to a decrease in experienced utility should be performed less often. According to economic theory, the probability of taking a particular action is going to be driven by one's estimate of decision utility for that action. Therefore, it can be hypothesised that we learn about the decision utilities for different actions through trial and error based on the experienced utility we obtained when taking those actions (or similar actions) in the past.

To get an idea about how this learning might take place we can introduce some ideas from a branch of computer science called reinforcement learning (Sutton and Barto, 1998). Reinforcement learning is concerned with building algorithms to enable artificial systems such as robots to learn adaptively from their environment, in order to increase the probability of robots learning through experience to take actions that lead to outcomes defined (by their designer) as positively reinforcing and avoid actions that are negatively reinforced. A key idea behind reinforcement learning is that learning occurs by comparing the agent's predictions about what is going to happen after taking a particular action, and what actually happens. The difference between what one expects to get and what one actually receives is formally known as a prediction error. The idea is that this prediction error is used to update the expectation or prediction (in essence the agent's decision utility) after every experience, so that cumulatively, over the course of a number of trials of experience, the prediction (synonymous with the decision utility) begins to converge on the actual experienced utility of the outcome.

The notion of learning through prediction errors was actually first proposed by the psychologists Robert Rescorla and Alan Wagner (1972), to explain how animals learned to become conditioned to particular stimuli, and this idea was then subsequently adopted by the developers of

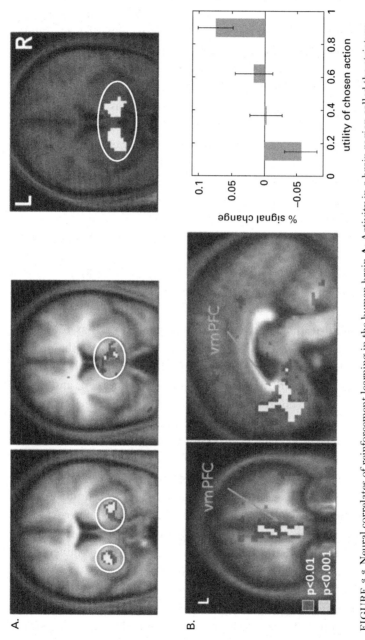

FIGURE 3.3 Neural correlates of reinforcement learning in the human brain **A:** Activity in a brain region called the striatum correlating with prediction errors during decision-making as measured with fMRI. Areas circled depict brain areas exhibiting significant correlations with the prediction error signal from a reinforcement learning model.
B: Activity in the ventromedial prefrontal cortex (vmPFC) correlating with the (decision) utility of the chosen action during performance of a simple decision-making task as measured with fMRI. The panel on the right shows average activity in this region plotted against a measure of the decision utility computed by a reinforcement-learning model.

reinforcement learning. Interest in the neurobiological relevance of the idea of a prediction error emerged following the observations of the Cambridge-based neuroscientist Wolfram Schultz (1998), who found that a certain group of neurons located deep in the brain that release a brain chemical called dopamine appear to behave very much like a prediction error signal from reinforcement learning should. These neurons increase their activity if a positive reinforcer (commonly called a reward) is delivered unexpectedly, don't respond when a reward is presented that is already predictable, and decrease their response if a reward is expected but unexpectedly not delivered (which would correspond to what is termed a negative prediction error, that is, when you expect something good to happen but it doesn't). Brain-imaging studies have revealed activity in regions of the brain where the dopamine carried by these neurons is released while people are learning to predict rewards from experience and making decisions (O'Doherty et al., 2004). The activity in these regions, most prominently in an area called the striatum which is located in the centre of the brain behind the frontal lobes, follows the pattern that would be expected for a prediction error from reinforcement learning (Figure 3.3). Thus, an influential hypothesis in contemporary neuroeconomics is that the way in which decision utilities are learned in the brain is by means of prediction errors which may be conveyed by the rapid neuronal firing patterns of dopamine neurons (Montague, Dayan and Sejnowski, 1996).

Decision utility

Now we can turn to where and how decision utilities are represented in the brain. To address this question we can put people in an fMRI scanner and ask them to make choices between different options. Nathanial Daw and colleagues (Daw et al., 2006) conducted just such an experiment. Subjects were asked to play a game called a four-armed bandit task (a name derived from the one-armed bandit slot machines found in casinos). In this task subjects are presented with four computer-generated slot machines, and all they have to do is choose one of them on each trial, after which they receive an outcome consisting of 'points' that they have won. Subjects are motivated to win as many points as possible and therefore they want to choose the bandit yielding the highest number of points. However, the number of points that can be won on each machine changes over time, so that while the 'red' machine may pay out more at the beginning of the experiment, later on the 'blue' machine may turn out to be best, and so on. Daw and colleagues used a reinforcement learning algorithm to estimate the subject's internal representations for the expected reward (or decision utility) that would follow from selecting each of the individual bandits according to past experience with those bandits (that is, the points obtained on previous trials when those bandits were selected). Daw et al. then tested for regions of the brain correlating with the decision utility of the action chosen on that trial as estimated by the reinforcement learning algorithm at the time that the volunteers were choosing the bandit, but before they obtained the outcome. Activity was found to correlate extensively with this measure of decision utility in the ventromedial prefrontal cortex (Figure 3.3B), the very same region as that found to produce impairments in decision-making in patients with damage to this area, from Phineas Gage to the present day. A role for the ventromedial prefrontal cortex in encoding decision utility has now been found during different types of decision-making tasks, and the same area appears to code for the decision utility for many different types of stimuli (or 'goods', as economists might call them), including decisions about monetary gambles or lotteries, decisions about immediate versus delayed rewards and decisions about food items, or even other consumer items such as clothing and DVDs, etc.

Decisions and risk

So far we have found evidence of a role for the ventromedial prefrontal cortex, incorporating the orbitofrontal cortex in encoding both decision and experience utilities. Although most decision-making that we have explored has taken place under conditions of uncertainty, and hence 'risk', we haven't yet addressed how the degree of riskiness in a choice might be actively incorporated into the decision process. Since the time of Bernoulli in the eighteenth century (Bernoulli, 1954), economists have appreciated that risk is an important feature in human decision-making. To appreciate this, imagine you are a participant in a TV game show and are given a choice between taking a gamble with a 50 per cent chance of winning £2,000 and a 50 per cent chance of winning nothing, or, alternatively, you can walk away with £1,000 for certain. Many people would prefer to take the certain option and not play the gamble, even though, if one were to play this game an infinite number of times, the average amount of money obtainable by playing the gamble (£1,000) is identical to the amount obtainable by taking the certain option (£1,000). What is going on here, is that those people favouring the certain option are exhibiting what is called risk-aversion – they prefer to stay away from the risky choice even if it is the same in terms of its overall value than the certain option. On the other hand, not everyone is risk-averse. In fact, some people are risk-seeking (as perhaps would be apparent from the interest that some people have in the pursuit of dangerous sports), and in the TV show scenario might be willing to plump for the risky gamble instead of the certain option. Risk-sensitivity is often viewed as a stable trait that differs reliably across individuals, although it should be noted that it is not necessarily the case that an individual showing risk-aversion in one domain will always be risk-averse in other domains (for example, I might be highly risk-averse when making decisions about money, but risk-seeking when it comes to trying out strange foods!).

Returning to the game-show example, we can now introduce an aspect of utility theory that we have hitherto glossed over. Bernoulli realised that one simple way to incorporate risk into the decision process was to assume that the utility of a particular good (such as a sum of money) was a non-linear rather than a linear function of the amount of the good available. This is shown in Figure 3.4 by plotting the amount of different possible winnings on the game show on the x-axis, against the subjective utility on the y-axis. What you can see from looking at the solid black line is that, rather than subjective utility necessarily being a linear function of the amount of money obtainable, here there is strong curvature in the function, so that the increase in subjective utility (or utils) corresponding to winning £2,000 compared to winning £1,000 is much less than the two times that would be expected based on the raw difference in monetary amount. Another way of thinking about this is that the difference in

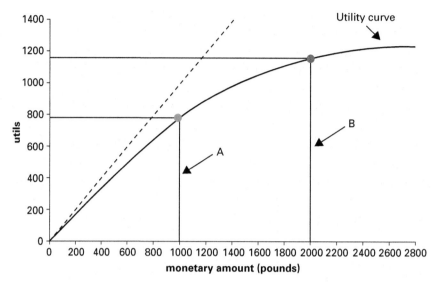

FIGURE 3.4 Illustration of a non-linear utility function capturing the risk preferences for a hypothetical individual. This individual would prefer to accept £1,000 for sure instead of a risky 50 per cent gamble of obtaining £2,000. Their preference is captured by the curve in the solid black line which reflects the relationship between that individual's subjective utility (y-axis) and the actual monetary amount being contemplated (on the x-axis). As can be seen by following the intersecting line marked 'A', the subjective utility of £1,000 corresponds to 790 'utils', whereas (following the intersecting line marked 'B') the subjective utility of £2,000 corresponds to approximately 1,180 utils. Multiplying the probability of the gamble by the utility of that gamble gives 0.5 × 1180 = 590 utils. Therefore, the utility of the sure bet is greater than that of the gamble, implying that this individual would prefer the sure bet, and would in general be risk-averse. On the other hand, if this individual's subjective utility was a purely linear function of the amount of money available (dashed line), then the utility of the gamble would be exactly twice that of the sure bet, implying that the individual would be 'risk-neutral', meaning that they would be equally likely to take the gamble or the sure bet. Finally, if the utility function were convex instead of concave (not shown here), the utility of the larger amount would end up being more than twice that of the smaller amount and this individual would, all else being equal, always opt for the risky gamble.

utility going from zero to £1,000 is much bigger than the difference in going from £1,000 to £2,000 even though the amount of increment is the same. The function shown in Figure 3.4 would produce risk-averse behaviour because, after multiplying the probability of winning against the subjective utility of the amount winnable, the expected utility of taking the safe option is greater than that of the risky one. By changing the degree of curvature of the utility curve it is possible to produce different types of patterns of risk-sensitivity, and while a concave curve (as shown) would produce risk-averse choices, a convex curve would actually produce risk-seeking choices. The beauty of this idea is that one can capture a whole range of choice behaviours using a single mathematically simple function. Unfortunately, as we mentioned in the introduction to this paper, people are not always consistent with this simple function in their actual choices, a finding that has prompted others to try to modify this framework in a variety of ways to make it fit better with actual choice behaviour (Kahneman and Tversky, 1979). An alternative (not necessarily mutually inconsistent) framework for thinking about risk is to propose that, rather than merely being reflected as the degree of curvature in a utility function, risk is actively computed as a variable in its own right and estimated and learned about from experience, similarly to how the utility itself might be learned (Preuschoff and Bossaerts, 2007).

Risk and the brain

In fact, there is now considerable evidence in support of the fact that risk is actually directly encoded in the brain, Preuschoff, Bossaerts and Quartz (2006) scanned volunteers with fMRI while they played a variant of a popular card gambling game in which an initial card was selected randomly from a deck of ten cards. After a delay, a second card was then drawn from the same deck. The second card will, of course, either be higher or lower than the first. At the beginning of the trial before any card decks are shown, the volunteers have to commit to a higher or lower decision. If the second card comes out according to their decision, then they win money. If not, they win nothing. After the reveal of the first card, the subject should be able to estimate (a) what the probability is that they will win, that is, what the probability is that the second card will be higher or lower (depending on their initial choice), and (b) what the risk is of this happening or not. It should be obvious if the first card is a 5 or a 6 then depending on whether one has opted for higher or lower, the probability of winning ranges from 4/9 to 5/9 and the risk

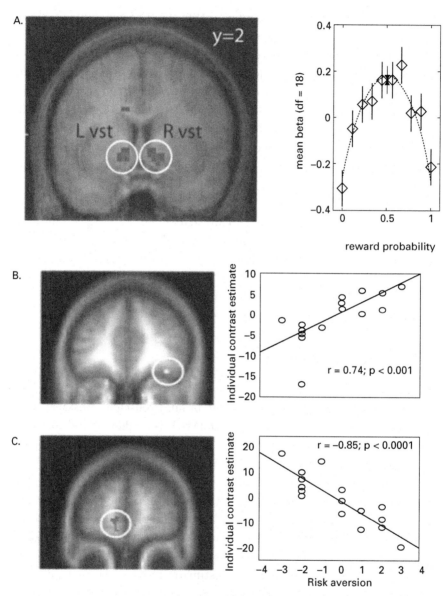

FIGURE 3.5 Areas of the brain correlating with risk. **A**: Anticipatory risk signals in the human brain. The brain image shows the location of risk signals in the striatum. The plot shows fMRI responses in this region as a function of reward probability, demonstrating a maximal response on trials when reward delivery is least predictable (i.e., with a probability p = 0.5), and a minimal response when the reward delivery is most predictable and is either certain to occur or not to occur (p = 0 and p = 1, respectively).

(or variance in the possible outcomes) is maximal. On the other hand, if one has opted for higher, and a 2 is drawn for the first card, then the probability of winning is 8/9 (88 per cent), and the risk in the outcome will be much lower than in the draw-5 case or draw-6. Similarly, if the subject had opted for lower and a 2 is drawn, the probability of winning is different at 1/9, but the variance in the outcome is identical to the case where the subject draws a 2 but had opted for higher. Mathematically, while the probability of winning corresponds to the expected value (or the mean) of the distribution of rewards, the risk function is the variance of the reward distribution (essentially a quadratic or inverted U-shaped function of the probability of winning). Preuschoff, Bossaerts and Quartz (2006) looked for areas of the brain correlating not only with expected value (in this case probability) but also with risk. They found activity correlating with risk in a number of brain regions, including the striatum (which we have encountered previously) and another brain area called the anterior insula. Activity in these areas on trials with different levels of risk looked very much like an inverted U-shaped response similar to the risk function itself, being highest on the draw-5 and draw-6 trials (when risk is maximum), and lowest on the draw-1 or draw-10 trials (where risk is minimal) (Figure 3.5A). These results suggest that risk is actually explicitly represented in the brain and is not exclusively represented as curvature in the utility function.

In order to investigate the influence of risk on neural utility signals, Philippe Tobler and colleagues (2007) looked for regions involved in responding to the expected value or utility of an outcome in which the response was modulated by the degree of risk-sensitivity exhibiting across

FIGURE 3.5 (*cont.*) **B**: Region of the medial prefrontal cortex in which activity in response to expected utility is increased the more risk-seeking an individual is, and decreased the more risk-averse an individual is (correlation between brain response and an individual's attitude to risk is shown in the right panel).

C: Region of the lateral orbitofrontal cortex correlating with expected utility showing the opposite type of modulation, i.e., the more risk-averse the individual was the greater the activity in this region in response to expected utility.

individuals. They found that the magnitude of the activity in the medial orbitofrontal cortex (part of the ventromedial prefrontal cortex) when contemplating the value of a particular decision option was modulated across individuals by the degree of risk-seeking exhibited by those individuals. Individuals who were more risk-seeking showed greater activation in this region in reponse to utility than individuals who were less risk-seeking, while activity in another part of the vmPFC showed the opposite pattern (activity increased the more risk-averse subjects were) (Figure 3.5B). Collectively these findings indicate that risk is encoded in the brain, and that one's attitude to risk (whether one is risk-seeking or risk-averse) is also reflected in the brain in the areas involved in actively encoding the utility signals necessary to compute decisions.

Outstanding questions

The field of neuroeconomics and the study of the neural basis of decision-making under uncertainty is still in its infancy. There are so many unanswered questions it would be impossible to do justice to them here. A really major question concerns understanding how separate representations of risk and decision utility come to be used to guide decision-making. One possibility is that they remain separate (that is, there is no explicit curvature in the neural utility function due to risk), but that the brain regions representing these two separate variables interact in order to produce risk-sensitive decision-making. Another question that has yet to be comprehensively answered is how precisely decision utilities for different options are actively compared in order ultimately to produce a decision. Although some ideas have been proposed, as yet definitive answers about how or even where decisions are computed have proved elusive. Another really fundamental question concerns how deviations or biases in human decision-making from that of a rational agent (as predicted by expected utility theory) are produced. Space has precluded review of these here, but many such biases have been documented. Clearly, there are some features of the machinery for decision-making in the brain that give rise to these biases, and understanding how such biases are produced is currently an active research area (de Martino et al., 2006).

Conclusion

In this paper I have given a broad introduction to the field of neuro-economics and reviewed the current state of knowledge about the brain mechanisms involved in computing some of the variables necessary for enabling good decisions to be made under conditions of uncertainty. These include decision and experienced utility, prediction errors by which experienced utility can be used to learn decision utilities through trial and error, and the degree of risk inherent in a choice. We found that a critical region for decision-making is the ventromedial prefrontal cortex, which appears to contain a representation not only of the experienced utility but also of the decision utility. Some other brain systems important for decision-making include the dopamine neurons deep in the midbrain that release high levels of dopamine in the striatum (among other places) during learning, as well as the anterior insula, which along with the striatum appears to encode representations of risk during decision-making. Much of the progress in understanding how decisions are computed in the brain has happened in the last twenty years, and the amount of research being conducted in this area has grown exponentially in this period. I would be willing to take a large risky bet on the prospect that the next twenty years will see even greater progress in elucidating the neural circuits underlying human decision-making.

References

Allais, M. (1953) 'Behaviour of the rational man before risk – criticism of American school postulates and axioms', *Econometrica* 21 (4): 503–46.

Bechara, A., Damasio, H. and Damasio, A. R. (2000) 'Emotion, decision-making and the orbitofrontal cortex', *Cerebral Cortex* 10 (3): 295–307.

Bechara, A., Damasio, A. R., Damasio, H. and Andersion, S. W (1994) 'Insensitivity to future consequences following damage to human prefrontal cortex', *Cognition* 50: 7–15.

Bentham, J. (1987) 'From an introduction to the principles of morals and legislation', in *Utilitarianism and Other Essays*, ed. J. S. Mill. Harmondsworth: Penguin Books.

Bernoulli, D. (1954) 'Exposition of a new theory on the measurement of risk', *Econometrica* 22 (1): 23–36.

Blood, A. J., Zatorre, R. J., Bermudez, P. and Evans, A. C. (1999) 'Emotional responses to pleasant and unpleasant music correlate with activity in paralimbic brain regions', *Nature Neuroscience* 2 (4): 382–7.

Damasio, H., Grabowski, T., Frank, R., Galaburda, A. M. and Damasio, A. R. (1994) 'The return of Phineas Gage: clues about the brain from the skull of a famous patient', *Science* 264 (5162): 1102–5.

Daw, N. D., O'Doherty, J. P., Dayan, P., Seymour, B. and Dolan, R. J. (2006) 'Cortical substrates for exploratory decisions in humans', *Nature* 441 (7095): 876–9.

de Araujo, I. E., Kringelbach, M. L., Rolls, E. T. and McGlone, F. (2003) 'Human cortical responses to water in the mouth, and the effects of thirst', *Journal of Neurophysiology* 90 (3): 1865–76.

de Araujo, I. E., Oliveira-Maia, A. J., Sotnikova, T. D., Gainetdinov, R. R., Caron, M. G., Nicolelis, M. A. L. and Simon, S. A. (2008) 'Food reward in the absence of taste receptor signaling', *Neuron* 57 (6): 930–41.

de Martino, B., Kumaran, D., Seymour, B. and Dolan, R. J. (2006) 'Frames, biases, and rational decision-making in the human brain', *Science* 313 (5787): 684–7.

Elliott, R., Newman, J. L., Longe, O. A. and Deakin, J. F. (2003) 'Differential response patterns in the striatum and orbitofrontal cortex to financial reward in humans: a parametric functional magnetic resonance imaging study', *Journal of Neuroscience* 23 (1): 303–7.

Glimcher, P. W., Camerer, C. F., Fehr, E. and Poldrack, R. A. (2009) 'Introduction: A brief history of neuroeconomics', in *Neuroeconomics: Decision-making and the Brain*, ed. P. W. Glimcher, C. F. Camerer, E. Fehr and R. A. Poldrack. London: Academic Press.

Grabenhorst, F. and Rolls, E. T. (2008) 'Selective attention to affective value alters how the brain processes taste stimuli', *European Journal of Neuroscience* 27 (3): 723–9.

Harlow, J. M. (1868) 'Recovery from the passage of an iron bar through the head', *Publications of the Massachusetts Medical Society* 2: 327–47.

Huettel, S., Song, A. and McCarthy, G. (2004) *Functional Magnetic Resonance Imaging*. Sunderland, MA: Sinauer Associates.

Kahneman, D. and Tversky, A. (1979) 'Prospect theory – an analysis of decision under risk', *Econometrica* 47 (2): 263–91.

Kahneman, D. and Tversky, A. (1984) 'Choices, values, and frames',
  American Psychologist 39 (4): 341–50.
Kahneman, D., Wakker, P. P. and Sarin, R. (1997) 'Back to Bentham? –
  Explorations of experienced utility', *Quarterly Journal of Economics*
  112 (2): 375–405.
Kim, H., Shimojo, S. and O'Doherty, J. P. (2006) 'Is avoiding an aversive
  outcome rewarding? Neural substrates of avoidance learning in the
  human brain', *PLoS Biology* 4 (8): e233.
Knutson, B., Fong, G. W., Adams, C. M., Varner, J. L. and Hommer, D.
  (2001) 'Dissociation of reward anticipation and outcome with
  event-related fMRI', *Neuroreport* 12 (17): 3683–7.
Montague, P. R., Dayan, P. and Sejnowski, T. J. (1996) 'A framework for
  mesencephalic dopamine systems based on predictive Hebbian
  learning', *Journal of Neuroscience* 16 (5): 1936–47.
O'Doherty, J., Kringelbach, M. L., Rolls, E. T., Hornak, J. and
  Andrews, C. (2001) 'Abstract reward and punishment
  representations in the human orbitofrontal cortex', *Nature
  Neuroscience* 4 (1): 95–102.
O'Doherty, J., Dayan, P., Schultz, J., Deichmann, R., Friston, K. and
  Dolan, R. J. (2004) 'Dissociable roles of ventral and dorsal
  striatum in instrumental conditioning', *Science* 304 (5669):
  452–4.
O'Doherty, J., Winston, J., Critchley, H., Perrett, D., Burt, D. M.
  and Dolan, R. J. (2003) 'Beauty in a smile: the role of medial
  orbitofrontal cortex in facial attractiveness', *Neuropsychologia* 41 (2):
  147–55.
O'Doherty, J., Rolls, E. T., Francis, S., Bowtell, R., McGlone, F., Kobal,
  G., Renner, B. and Ahne, G. (2000) 'Sensory-specific satiety-related
  olfactory activation of the human orbitofrontal cortex', *Neuroreport*
  11 (4): 893–7.
Plassmann, H., O'Doherty, J., Shiv, B. and Rangel, A. (2008) 'Marketing
  actions can modulate neural representations of experienced
  pleasantness', *Proceedings of the National Academy of Sciences USA* 105
  (3): 1050–4.
Preuschoff, K. and Bossaerts, P. (2007) 'Adding prediction risk to the
  theory of reward learning', *Annals of the New York Academy of
  Sciences* 1104: 135–46.
Preuschoff, K., Bossaerts, P. and Quartz, S. R. (2006) 'Neural
  differentiation of expected reward and risk in human subcortical
  structures', *Neuron* 51 (3): 381–90.
Rescorla, R. A. and Wagner, A. R. (1972) 'A theory of Pavlovian
  conditioning: variations in the effectiveness of reinforcement and

nonreinforcement', in *Classical Conditioning II: Current Research and Theory*, ed. A. H. Black and W. F. Prokasy, pp. 64–99. New York: Appleton Crofts.

Schultz, W. (1998) 'Predictive reward signal of dopamine neurons', *Journal of Neurophysiology* 80 (1): 1–27.

Smith, V. L. (1982) 'Microeconomic systems as an experimental science', *American Economic Review* 72 (5): 923–55.

Steiner, J. E., Glaser, D., Hawilo, M. E. and Berridge, K. C. (2001) 'Comparative expression of hedonic impact: affective reactions to taste by human infants and other primates', *Neuroscience and Biobehavioural Reviews* 25 (1): 53–74.

Sutton, R. S. and Barto, A. G. (1998) *Reinforcement Learning: An Introduction*. Cambridge, MA: MIT Press.

Thorndike, E. L. (1898) 'Animal intelligence: an experimental study of the associative processes in animals', *Psychological Review*, Monograph Supplements, No. 8, New York: Macmillan.

Tobler, P. N., O'Doherty, J. P., Dolan, R. J. and Schultz, W. (2007) 'Reward value coding distinct from risk attitude-related uncertainty coding in human reward systems', *Journal of Neurophysiology* 97 (2): 1621–32.

Von Neumann, J. and Morgenstern, O. (1944) *Theory of Games and Economic Behaviour*. Princeton University Press.

Further reading

Camerer, C. F. (2008) 'Neuroeconomics: opening the gray box', *Neuron* 60 (3): 416–19.

Glimcher, P. W. and Rustichini, A. (2004) 'Neuroeconomics: the consilience of brain and decision', *Science* 306 (5695): 447–52.

Glimcher, P. W., Camerer, C. F., Fehr, E. and Poldrack, R. A. (2009) *Neuroeconomics: Decision-making and the Brain*. London: Academic Press.

Knutson, B. and Bossaerts P. (2007) 'Neural antecedents of financial decisions', *Journal of Neuroscience* 27 (31): 8174–7.

Knutson, B. and Cooper, J. C. (2005) 'Functional magnetic resonance imaging of reward prediction', *Current Opinion Neurology* 18 (4): 411–72.

O'Doherty, J. P. (2004) 'Reward representations and reward-related learning in the human brain: insights from neuroimaging', *Current Opinion Neurobiology* 14 (6): 769–76.

O'Doherty, J. P., Hampton, A. and Kim, H. (2007) 'Model-based fMRI and its application to reward learning and decision making', *Annals of the New York Academy of Sciences* 1104: 35–53.

Rangel, A., Camerer, C. and Montague, P. R. (2008) 'A framework for studying the neurobiology of value-based decision making', *Nature Reviews Neuroscience* 9 (7): 545–56.

4 Risk and government

The architectonics of blame-avoidance

CHRISTOPHER HOOD

Puzzling over gaps between practice and declared principles in government and public services

It is often said that high officeholders in government, both elected and appointed, live chronically time-pressured lives with many urgent and competing claims crowding in on their limited time and attention. Such individuals often, indeed routinely, declare that they want to focus on the big picture and on the pursuit of their grand visions, and that they are mainly concerned with achieving results that bring substantive social value rather than with small-print details of process and structure or with the trivialities of day-to-day media gossip.

Yet careful analysis of how those high-level officeholders in government use their limited time often reveals that they spend a remarkably large proportion of it – 50 per cent or more, on some estimates – on matters of media presentation[1] and that they often devote a surprising amount of their time as well to small-print details of legislation and government organisation.[2]

We find a similar disjuncture when it comes to the structure and operation of organisations in government and public services. Much has been said about the desirability of transparency and clear lines of accountability, of 'joined-up' operations that avoid underlaps and overlaps among different units and organisations, and of high-intelligence regulation that is clearly focused on results and closely proportioned to levels of risk. Yet when we look at government and public services in practice we find that, in spite of costly public-service reforms, responsibility for adverse outcomes

---

[1] See for instance Kurtz 1998: 24.
[2] See for instance Dunleavy and White 2010; Pollitt 1984: ix.

is often highly elusive when 'the shit hits the fan'; that responsibilities for dealing with risk are often dispersed among multiple organisations and levels of government that pass the buck to one another when individuals try to cope with everyday risk problems and battle with unhelpful helplines and impenetrable customer relations systems; and that regulation of many kinds of risk, from airport security to child-minding among friends, is often rigidly bureaucratic and inflexible in practice.

Where blame-avoidance comes in and shapes the handling of risk

There are, of course, various ways of accounting for those often-observed gaps between what is professed and what seems to be practised both by top-level leaders and by so many organisations in executive government and public services. But it is the way that the pursuit of blame-avoidance contributes to such outcomes that this chapter aims to explore.

The argument here is that:

1. Attempts to avoid blame by politicians and appointed government officials often – not always – trump other concerns in the conduct and structuring of government in general and the handling of risk more particularly, because the sort of risk that ordinarily tends to matter most in government is the risk of blame.[3]
2. The blame-avoidance imperative often applies as much, if not more, to the behaviour of appointed officials in government as to that of elected politicians, and it often extends to private or independent sector providers of public services as well.
3. Not all efforts to avoid blame lead to successful blame-avoidance, but attempts to avoid blame can powerfully shape structure, process and activity in government, in ways that can be positive as well as negative.

So this chapter aims to explore the 'architectonics' of blame-avoidance in government, using the term architectonics in two of its senses – the

---

[3] I say 'ordinarily' because plainly there are some circumstances in which blame-avoidance is not the paramount concern of officeholders or organisations, for instance when things get so bad that people stop worrying about blame and concentrate on their own physical survival by any means possible. But such circumstances are assumed to be extremes rather than normal cases.

sense of the underlying structure and design of government and how it is shaped by blame-avoidance concerns, and the Kantian sense of systematic knowledge. We begin with some basic concepts and definitions, proceed to an analysis of three main types of blame-avoidance activity, and conclude with a discussion of the positive and negative aspects of blame-avoidance for the conduct of government in general and for the handling of risk in particular.

Some basic concepts and definitions: blame, blame games, blame risk and blame-avoidance

Blame

Blame is conventionally taken to be the act of attributing something considered to be bad or wrong to some person or entity. Formally, it can be expressed as $B_{t1} = PAH_{t1} + PR_{t1}$

> Where:
> B = blame
> PAH = perceived avoidable harm or loss
> PR = perceived responsibility
> t = time

The two basic elements involved in blame are thus some perceived avoidable harm or loss (PAH, something that some person or group sees as worse than it could have been if matters had been handled better or differently) and some attribution of agency or responsibility (PR, an individual, organisation, set of organisations or some more abstract entity[4] that some person or group sees as having caused PAH by acts of commission or omission). But both of those elements, PAH and PR, can change over time, and time is often crucial to blame. Culpability often turns on precisely when something happened, and in politics and bureaucracy the killer career-ending question is often 'when did you know . . . ?' Moreover, an act that attracts blame at one point in time can attract praise at a later time, or vice versa.

Of course we can blame ourselves for avoidable harms or losses, and indeed there is a substantial literature on 'self-blame' in psychology. But

---

[4] Such as 'patriarchy' or 'the Establishment'.

the analysis here focuses only on blame as a social or political process, not self-blame. As a social process, blaming must involve at least two sets of actors, those who do the blaming (the blame-makers, so to speak) and those who are on the receiving end (blame-takers). And indeed blaming is often central to social and political life, which tends to consist of subcultures engaged in mutual blaming about what they see as the defects of each other's beliefs and ways of life.[5]

Why and when does blame matter? Some individuals can seem impervious to blame, while others are totally preoccupied with it. And blame can vary in its consequences, from mild social embarrassment, though serious career, financial or reputational damage, to loss of liberty and even life in extreme cases. But the risk of blame is usually a central preoccupation in politics and bureaucracy, for several reasons. One is that the occupational imperative of politicians and bureaucrats is usually understood as a tendency to seek credit and avoid blame in the pursuit of their careers. So such individuals will seek to minimise risks of damaging their careers or reducing their chances of re-election. Second, even in circumstances where there is no totally blame-free option, such individuals can usually be expected to aim for the course that attracts the least (or the least damaging) blame.

And third, avoiding the risk of blame can outweigh the chance of obtaining credit if there is strong 'negativity bias'. The term negativity bias is only one of various names for the commonly observed human cognitive tendency for more attention to be paid to negative than to positive information and for losses to be valued more highly than gains of an equivalent amount (commonly between two and four times more highly according to a number of studies).[6] In politics, action (such as turnout, vote choice or switching among parties) is often prompted more by hatred, dislike or dissatisfaction than by friendship or satisfaction, and politicians often get less credit from the voters for their successes than the blame they get for failures.[7] Similarly, media treatments of public policy

[5] Douglas 1990.   [6] See Heath, Larrick and Wu, 1999.
[7] See for example Borraz 2007: 226, on the electoral fortunes of French municipalities grappling with change to France's traditional practice of using sewage sludge as agricultural fertiliser; and James and John 2007 and Boyne et al. 2010 on the electoral fortunes of incumbents in English local authorities relative to their score on standard performance indicators.

developments often focus on the negatives rather than the positives.[8] Politicians can suffer severe career damage when they fail to identify or correctly estimate the strength of negativity bias. That happened to Margaret Thatcher after she failed to calculate that the losers from her 1989 poll tax would be more voluble than the gainers, even though the gainers were more numerous than the losers,[9] and to Jacques Chirac after he failed to anticipate that the 2005 referendum on a new European Union constitution would be seized upon by those who wanted to express discontent with his rule rather than by those who admired his bold vision of greater European unity.

Negativity bias is often at the heart of bureaucratic behaviour too, and for the same sort of reasons – because media, legislative committees, auditors and watchdogs, and political and bureaucratic masters tend to pay far more attention to the failures of bureaucrats and bureaucracies than to their successes. The so-called 'fire-alarm' approach to controlling bureaucratic behaviour by legislatures (that is, an approach to control, which works by acting on the basis of alarm bells rather than routine monitoring like police patrols) is well established in both theory[10] and practice, and it acts as a powerful incentive for blame-avoidance. That is why 'risk-aversion' (or more accurately blame-aversion) has long been noted as a common trait in bureaucratic behaviour. It is why it makes sense for blame-avoidance to trump credit-claiming when the two things come into conflict. And it is why it often seems to pay better to be average than to try to be excellent.

Blame games

The phrase 'blame game' has become widely used in recent years, usually as a term of opprobrium, to denote a situation in which the role of blame-makers and blame-takers intersect, as two or more players try to pin the responsibility on one another for some event or action involving perceived harm or loss. Blame games occur when the players act as blamers in their efforts to avoid being blamees, and the tone of much commentary about such activity is to portray it as somewhat disreputable. The implication is that the world of government and risk management would be better off

[8] See for instance Hood and Dixon 2010.
[9] See Butler, Adonis and Travers 1994.   [10] McCubbins and Schwartz 1984.

FIGURE 4.1 'Playing the blame game'.

without blame games, if only lines of responsibility could be made more clear-cut and individuals could bring themselves to acknowledge fault more openly.

Blame games in that sense are commonly observable. They feature in innumerable jokes and cartoons, and they can take several forms. They can occur inside an organisation, for instance when the corporate hierarchy blames individual front-line operators for mistakes, and those individuals in turn blame poor management or systems for creating the conditions in which errors are inevitable. They can occur between organisations or levels of government, for example when responsibility for some perceived harm or loss can be disputed because multiple institutional players are involved. They can occur before the event (when individuals or organisations try to 'get their retaliation in first')[11] or after it, when the

[11] An example of the anticipative kind of blame game arose in January 2010 in the United States, when the Democrats lost what had previously been the rock-solid Democrat Senate seat of Massachusetts, and the mutual blaming between the party's Senatorial candidate, Martha Coakley, the central party apparatus and the

pressure is on to find a scapegoat for some adverse event, such as the failures that led up to the financial crashes of the late 2000s, the responses to the 2004 Indian ocean earthquake and resulting tsunami, the handling of the aftermath of Hurricane Katrina in New Orleans in 2005, or the massive oil spill in the Gulf of Mexico in 2010 after an explosion on BP's 'Deepwater Horizon' oil rig and the failure of the blowout preventer on the underwater oil well it was drilling. The complex world of modern organisations and executive government, with its impenetrable intergovernmental arrangements and highly fragmented structures of sub-contracting, elaborate partnership arrangements and separation of delivery and commissioning agencies, provides plenty of scope for blame games in that sense, and indeed provides reasons for such behaviour. For instance, in the case of the Deepwater Horizon disaster mentioned above, complex blame issues arose around the rigour of the regulatory regime that allowed and encouraged deepwater oil drilling in a sensitive ecosystem at the limits of technological capacity, BP's practices that led to the explosion and fire on the drilling rig and its supervision of its numerous sub-contractors, the failure of the blowout preventer installed by one of its sub-contractors and the cementing work on the oil well conducted by another. Resolving issues of blame in such situations where there are multiple actors and high corporate and political stakes almost inevitably results in a process of claim and counter-claim.

Blame risk and blame-avoidance

Blame risk is the perceived likelihood that blame, as defined above, will occur – or that the combination of $PAH_{t1} + PR_{t1}$, as defined above, will occur. As suggested above, the risk of blame is normally a central preoccupation in politics and bureaucracy and it consequently tends to shape the way all other types of risks are handled. So to understand the handling of risk in other senses in government and politics, we have to understand how blame risk is handled.[12]

White House was in full swing several days before the polls closed: biggovernment.com/2010/01/19/coakley-blame-game-in-full-swing/#idc-cover, comment posted by 'ALLAMERICAN', 20 January 2010 (accessed January 2010).
[12] See Hood, Rothstein and Baldwin 2001.

The phrase 'blame-avoidance' has been in currency in political science for over twenty years, though the idea behind it has been in the literature of politics and government for centuries. For instance in the early sixteenth century Niccolò Machiavelli[13] famously observed in *The Prince* that 'princes should give rewards and favours with their own hands but death and punishment at the hands of others', and three hundred years later Jeremy Bentham in his 1820 *Constitutional Code* observed in exasperation that in the system of government Britain had at that time, 'No one is responsible for any thing that he does.'[14]

The term 'blame-avoidance' in modern political science parlance is conventionally attributed to the work of Kent Weaver (of Georgetown University in Washington) in the 1980s. Weaver began his seminal article with the apparently puzzling observation that elected politicians in the USA – and he thought in other countries as well – often tended to prefer avoiding blame to claiming credit, and thus passed up credit-claiming opportunities when the chance of gaining credit had to be set against the risk of blame.[15] Weaver linked this blame-avoidance observation to the phenomenon of 'retrospective voting' that was beginning to attract attention in political science at that time – that is, the tendency of voters to base their electoral choices on the past record of a candidate or party rather than on its promises or plans for the future. He also linked the observation to the idea of negativity bias, as discussed earlier.

When Weaver made this observation, similar themes were emerging from writing about social psychology and social choice theory, in particular with the classic work of Daniel Kahneman and Amos Tversky on risk asymmetry.[16] Over the subsequent decades, the blame-avoidance perspective has been developed in political science in several ways. For instance, there is a vein of writing about welfare state cutbacks (highly relevant to present political circumstances) that looks at how incumbent politicians manage welfare reductions to limit their risk of electoral punishment from voters, for example by careful salami-slicing that avoids giving labour unions very clear-cut issues about which they might march

---

[13] Machiavelli 1961: 106.   [14] Bentham 1983: 180.   [15] Weaver 1986 and 1988.
[16] Kahneman and Tversky 1979.

on May Day demonstrations,[17] or by 'grandfathering' arrangements that divide generations of beneficiaries.

Some analysis of blame-avoidance has aimed to go beyond Weaver's fairly discursive analysis, for example by experimental studies of responses to vignettes,[18] and by attempts to quantify levels of media blame over time to explore the effect of any of officeholders' responses.[19] And the blame-avoidance perspective has been applied to policy fields other than those originally considered by Weaver, for example health risks,[20] and financial risks,[21] to show how risk management is shaped by efforts to avoid blame. So blame-avoidance is now a developing theme in political science, and it cuts across three strands of the subject that usually live in different epistemic boxes – namely the analysis of institutional architectonics (why institutions are designed the way that they are), the analysis of policy processes (how policy-making and implementation works) and the working of electoral processes and public opinion.

Forms of blame-avoidance

Blame-avoidance can take several forms. For example, we can distinguish between blame-avoidance as activity and blame-avoidance as outcome; we can distinguish between anticipative and reactive types of blame-avoidance activity; and we can distinguish between presentational, agency and policy types of blame-avoidance.

Blame avoidance as activity and as outcome

Sometimes confusingly, the term blame-avoidance is used to denote both activity and outcomes – the activity of attempting to avoid or reduce blame, and outcomes that involve the absence, deflection or mitigation of blame. But of course we need to distinguish between outcome and activity, because to attempt blame-avoidance is one thing and to achieve it is quite another, as numerous studies of officeholders and organisations

---

[17] See Lindbom 2007. [18] McGraw 1990; Sulitzeanu-Kenan 2006.
[19] Hood et al. 2009. [20] Hood, Rothstein and Baldwin 2001. [21] Black 2005.

"Shifting the paradigm didn't work. Time for
Plan B...shifting the blame."

FIGURE 4.2 'Reactive blame avoidance' from www.CartoonStock.com.

attempting to deflect blame have shown.[22] Indeed, the very activity of
blame-avoidance may itself act as a blame magnet, as happened to the
propaganda machines of both Bill Clinton and Tony Blair.

Blame-avoidance as anticipation and reaction, and as harm-related and responsibility-related activity

Following the definition of blame offered earlier, as a combination of
perceived harm and perceived responsibility at a given point in time, it
follows that blame-avoidance can be concentrated on reducing perceptions
of harm or on reducing perceptions of responsibility (or both) and that
such activity can be conducted at different times.

Taking the time element first, we can distinguish between anticipative
and reactive blame-avoidance measures.[23] Anticipative blame-avoidance

---

[22] For example McGraw 1990 suggested that some types of blame-avoidance activity (justifications) were more effective than others (excuses) in achieving blame-
avoidance outcomes; Sultizeanu-Kenan 2006 suggested that public inquiries were
limited as a device for blame-avoidance because of the effect of 'conditional credi-
bility'; and Hood et al. 2009 showed that ministerial efforts to avoid blame in two
cases had only limited effect on the level of blame in the media.

[23] Sulitzeanu-Kenan and Hood 2005.

Table 4.1 *Four basic types of blame-avoidance*

Blame element	Time element	
	Anticipative	Reactive
Limit perception of harm (PAH)	(1) Example: Stressing likely losses or harms in advance, so that there is a sense of 'reprieve' when outcomes turn out to be less bad	(2) Example: talking down the extent of harm or loss incurred after the event
Limit perception of responsibility (PR)	(3) Example: stressing the inevitability of adverse events in advance (e.g. terrorist attack) so that they can be presented as 'nobody's fault' when they occur	(4) Example: denying responsibility, buck-passing or blame-sharing

seeks to stop blame before it starts, for instance by the well-known tactic of 'pre-buttal', or pre-emptive retaliation when blame is to be expected. Reactive blame-avoidance means responding to blame after it has emerged, as the emergency services go out to deal with accidents or mishaps after they have occurred.

When we combine the harm/responsibility distinction in blame-avoidance with the anticipation/reaction distinction, we get the four logical possibilities that are given in Table 4.1.

All of these types of blame avoidance can readily be observed in practice, as the examples indicate. And in principle, strategic choice in blame-avoidance can be understood as where to put the balance of activity among the four elements of Table 4.1 in what conditions, in order to avoid or minimise blame.

Presentational, agency and policy strategies of blame-avoidance

Another way of think about different approaches to blame-avoidance is by distinguishing the means used to pursue the approaches denoted in Table 4.1. From the scattered literature on the subject, we can distinguish among presentational strategies, agency strategies and policy strategies.[24]

Presentational strategies are those strategies that focus on changing or shaping perceptions, often of harm, but sometimes of responsibility too. Central to presentational strategy is framing, rhetorical and spin-doctoring activity, as encapsulated in the saying that 'the best way to deal with nuclear waste is to hire a PR company'.[25]

Agency strategies are those strategies that focus on organisational structures and the allocation of officeholders to portfolios, mainly to deal with the responsibility element of blame. Central to agency strategy are forms of delegation, jurisdictional boundaries and partnership arrangements, for example when toxic policy responsibilities are delegated to arm's-length agencies following a blame crisis (as happened in the UK over food safety after the BSE crisis of the 1990s and over responsibilities for border control after the release-of-foreign-prisoners crisis of the mid-2000s).

Policy or operational strategies are those strategies that focus on the policy choices that organisations make and the standard operating routines they follow, again mainly to deal with the responsibility element of blame. A well-known example is the practice of so-called defensive medicine, a term originally coined in the United States in the late 1960s to denote the practice of medicine in a manner primarily designed to avoid the risk of malpractice suits by a mixture of what is called assurance and avoidance behaviour.[26] Avoidance behaviour is the avoidance of high-risk patients (such as medical malpractice lawyers or their relatives), while assurance behaviour is the pursuit of every possible diagnostic or therapeutic option or the following of standard protocols in every case to reduce the risk of allegations of negligence. Analogous practices are often to be found in other public services as well, such as in defensive social work and defensive education.

Combinations and varieties

In general, agency and policy strategies for blame-avoidance appear to be best fitted for anticipative application. Because they require enactment

---

[24] Hood 2002.   [25] *Private Eye*, No. 1144 (28 Oct.–10 Nov. 2005): 26.
[26] See *Duke Law Journal* 1971.

of structures or procedures, they are harder to use after a blame crisis starts, whereas presentational strategies can be used both anticipatively and reactively. An example of anticipative use of such strategies, as noted in Table 4.1, is the case of efforts to lower expectations or deny responsibility in advance, for instance when police chiefs declare that major terrorist incidents are inevitable or that the breakdown of social discipline makes crime unavoidable and is therefore not the fault of the police. But presentational strategies can also be used reactively in the midst of a blame firestorm. That process is vividly captured by Paul Flynn's epigram (originally a comment on the machinations of the Labour government in Wales in the late 1990s) that 'Only the future is certain. The past is always changing.'[27] That all-purpose nature of presentational strategies is perhaps the reason why government leaders and top politicians tend to spend so much time on them.

Each of these three types of blame-avoidance can be broken down into multiple variants. For instance, in the case of presentational strategies, we can distinguish between the sort of spin or rhetorical activity that is designed to win arguments over blame – by making a plausible case to mitigate perceptions of responsibility (PR) or by offering justifications designed to mitigate perceptions of harm or loss (PAH) – from those that work in some other way. Three of those other ways are non-engagement (the empty-chair or no-comment strategy so often employed by beleaguered individuals or organisations in the midst of a blame episode), diversionary tactics or changing the subject (the well-known tactic of finding good days, such as public holidays or major sports events, to bury bad news) and by drawing-a-line approaches in which leaders concede that 'mistakes have been made' (often in that so-called 'past exonerative tense', which is said to date back at least to the nineteenth century) but then seek to draw a line under whatever it was and hurriedly move on.

Agency strategies also comprise multiple variants. For instance, we can distinguish between simple delegation, in which responsibilities are passed from one organisation or actor to another in a clear-cut way, from other ways of shaping perceptions of responsibility. Those other ways include defensive reorganisation, management or ministerial

---

[27] Flynn 1999: 24.

merry-go-rounds[28] that allow current incumbents to deny responsibility for what happened under previous structures or officeholders, and complex intergovernmental arrangements or partnership arrangements (such as public–private partnerships over major sporting events) that make it hard to attribute responsibility among a group of organisations that can blame one another when things go wrong.

Policy strategies come in many different forms as well. As noted earlier, the literature on defensive medicine identifies what have been called 'assurance' and 'avoidance' strategies for limiting the risks of malpractice suits against doctors, the first involving a heavy emphasis on rule-following and standard protocols rather than the exercise of (contestable) discretion, and the second involving decisions not to treat high-risk groups or to offer high-risk services. But there are other policy strategies that can be used in attempts to avoid blame, such as the 'disclaimer' approach of putting the onus of responsibility over risk on to individual users or operators (either in small print or in large print), and the 'herding' approach of making every decision by teams or groups such that blame cannot be pinned on any one individual.

At the margin, of course, presentational, agency and policy strategies merge into one another, for example when organisation is so plastic that agency strategies and presentational strategies cannot readily be distinguished. But the point of this brief analysis is to show, first, that there are several roads to blame-avoidance in government and politics, not just one; and second, that once we start thinking along the lines sketched out above, we can identify a whole logic of how to design policy and operating routines in risk management, how to structure organisations and how to handle information, that runs clean counter to those orthodox precepts about good organisation and policy in government that conveniently assume away blame risk and negativity bias. And that in turn can help us to understand why regimes for handling risk that seem to make so little sense from an orthodox good governance perspective (for example where responsibility is diffuse and defensiveness reigns in spite of a pervasive rhetoric of clear-cut accountability and risk-based

---

[28] Much criticised by the Better Government Initiative 2010 and by many previous reports.

proportionality) can make perfect sense if we take attempts to avoid blame risk as the underlying, if unstated, logic of design.[29]

Does it matter? The wrong sort of blame-avoidance

What are the normative or what-to-do issues raised by this little analysis? As was noted earlier, blame, blame-avoidance and 'blame games' – mutual blaming among individuals or organisations trying to disclaim responsibility for some perceived harm or loss – generally get a bad press. They are a favourite target of media attacks, satirical jokes and even of most academic work, the tone of which is almost invariably to frown on blame games and blame-avoidance as a dysfunctional, unheroic and rather unsavoury aspect of politics and bureaucracy that the world would be better off without. 'Blame cultures' tend to be castigated by politicians, commentators and public managers as something we need to get away from into the sort of world inhabited by the superheroes of popular culture. Social conversations about the subject very often take the same tone. As with social conflict generally, few people have a good word to say for blame games.

But just as the sociologist Lewis Coser many years ago pointed to some positive functions of social conflict,[30] this often implicit or semi-explicit view of blame-avoidance can be challenged. A more balanced view of the subject would point to some of the positive features of blame as a social phenomenon, of blame games as a social and political activity and even of some kinds of blame-avoidance activity in the handling of risk.

On this more nuanced view, blame and the desire to avoid blame can have some distinctly positive social and political effects. The fear of blame is a central regulator of human conduct and it can lead individuals to follow rules and conventions and to observe social restraints in a way that they would not otherwise do. A so-called 'blame culture' may have some obvious disadvantages, as highlighted by all the jokes and strictures noted above, but if we imagine the opposite – a wholly no-blame culture – such a social world would be likely to be far from problem-free. Where and

---

[29] Hood, Rothstein and Baldwin 2001.   [30] Coser 1956.

what would be the incentives for individuals to take care about how they behaved, what they said to whom, how they conducted their personal and professional lives? Would a world in which those who rule or administer us never had to fear any blame be any better governed than one in which their every action has to be conducted in the shadow of blame risk? Blame, or more strictly the fear of blame, can sometimes act as a powerful force to check carelessness, self-gratification and disregard for the views of others.

'Blame games' – in the sense defined earlier of mutual blaming among two or more potential blamees – can have positive effects as well, even though they often get, if anything, a worse press than the much-castigated 'blame culture'. But 'blame-game' activity, far from being a purely dysfunctional social process, can perform a social discovery function about the attribution of responsibility for avoidable harms in complex institutional settings that are hard to achieve in any other way.

What sort of circumstances make blame games necessary as discovery mechanisms for pinning down responsibility for harm? Such activity would perhaps not be needed in a world where responsibility could be established by contingent contracting or by the application of superior technical expertise. Contingent contracting – the attempt to spell out in formal *ex ante* contracts who exactly is to be responsible for what in a range of possible circumstances – is limited by the ability to foresee all the relevant circumstances that could possibly arise. Leaving the job of assigning blame and responsibility to technical experts is similarly limited by the point at which the lack of available data, or disagreements among the relevant scientists or professionals, prevents definitive evaluation of that sort. So blame games are needed as a social mechanism for settling questions of harm and responsibility if only because the legalistic write-down-everything-in-advance approach and the technocratic leave-it-to-the-experts evaluation approach are so often inapplicable. However messy and undignified the process of mutual blaming may be in the glare of media attention, such processes can in fact perform an educative and discovery function, just as Friedrich Hayek thought markets had a value as discovery systems over costs and prices.[31]

[31] Hayek 1978.

Finally, it can be argued that blame-avoidance behaviour is not necessarily all bad either. Of course there are some obvious dysfunctions that can follow from preoccupations with blame-avoidance, when blame risks shape the way that every other kind of risk is handled. For instance, such a preoccupation can result in shifting the burden of responsibility for adverse outcomes from corporations and governments on to individual users or operators who may be worse placed to assess and manage the risks involved. It can even result in exposing individuals to higher levels of risk to life and limb if that means lower corporate or governmental blame risk. For instance, if rural passenger railway lines are shut down because they generate insufficient revenue to justify installing the very latest state-of-the-art signalling systems, railway companies or governments may reduce their exposure to possible blame or litigation for not installing such systems in the event of a crash. But at the same time the passengers involved are likely to be exposed to much higher risks of death or injury if they have to make their journeys by road.[32] Similarly, critics of the behaviour that is associated with the practice of defensive medicine, claim that such behaviour greatly increases the overall costs of health care (whether those costs are met from general taxation or insurance charges) and that it can expose individuals to greater health risk as a result of the damage that over-testing can do to them (for example from X-rays or CT scans). Similar criticisms can be made about the effects of avoidance behaviour, for example in reluctance to treat high-risk patients with complex conditions.

But it can still be argued that blame-avoidance activity does not invariably have wholly dysfunctional effects for governance and risk management. Rather, as Andrea Prat has suggested for transparency,[33] it can be argued that there can be 'the wrong kind of blame avoidance', but also that there can be positive kinds. Harking back to the earlier discussion of blame, blame-avoidance activity can have positive social effects for governance or risk management if it leads people to take more care, or practise more self-restraint, than they would otherwise do. It can likewise have positive effects if it encourages politicians and top leaders of various kinds to delegate responsibilities for matters of technical judgement or detailed

---

[32] See NERA 2000: 85 n. 57.   [33] Prat 2005.

Table 4.2 *The wrong kind of blame-avoidance?*

Type of strategy	Criteria for assessment		
	Sharpen or blunt policy debate	Focus or diffuse accountability	Increase or decrease transparency
Presentational strategies	Avoiding argument variants		
Agency strategies		Muddying-waters variants	
Policy and operational strategies			Herding and disclaimer variants

programme management to people who are better fitted than they are to carry out those functions and answer for what they do. Sometimes it can even lead to more balanced debate and better understanding of policy or administrative issues or matters of personal conduct, as officeholders seeking to avoid blame in the face of onslaughts from the media or other critics put the best gloss they can on their side of the story and bring out the difficulty or complexity of the choices or actions they have to take.

So rather than focus exclusively on the negative aspects of blame-avoidance activity, it can be argued that each of the three main types of blame-avoidance strategy discussed earlier (that is, presentational strategies, agency strategies and policy strategies) can be positive in some of their variants but negative in other variants. Positivity or negativity could be judged in various ways, but here it is taken to mean how far blame-avoidance approaches are conducive to three important criteria for good governance, namely whether they serve to sharpen policy debate (as against blunting it), whether they focus accountability (as against diffusing it), and whether they increase transparency (as against decreasing it).

Tables 4.2 and 4.3 illustrate this argument. For presentational strategies, those variants that are designed to engage in arguments – by offering persuasive excuses or justifications for why something was done or not done – can be considered positive against the first criterion (sharpening

Table 4.3 *The right kind of blame-avoidance?*

Type of strategy	Criteria for assessment		
	Sharpen or blunt policy debate	Focus or diffuse accountability	Increase or decrease transparency
Presentational strategies	Winning argument variants		
Agency strategies		Simple delegation variants	
Policy and operational strategies			Abstinence and rule-following variants

policy debate), while presentational strategies that are designed to evade arguments by changing the subject or killing debate by non-engagement are negative. For agency strategies, those variants that involve clear-cut delegation of authority can be considered positive against the second criterion (focusing accountability), while those variants that are designed to muddy the waters of perceived responsibility (for instance by defensive reorganisation or officeholder merry-go-rounds) are negative. For policy strategies, those variants that involve attempts to avoid blame by strict protocolisation, or even by clear decisions not to provide certain services that may attract blame, can be considered positive against the third criterion (increasing transparency), while those policy strategies that involve masking blame by group decision-making are negative. In short, there can be good as well as bad forms of blame-avoidance.

Conclusion

The argument advanced here about government and the management of risk is threefold, namely:

1.   That to understand properly how government manages risk, it is necessary to pay attention to the risk that ordinarily matters most in government and bureaucracy, namely the risk of blame.

2. That attempts to control the risk of blame can take multiple forms rather than a single one, with at least three major strategies and numerous variations of each strategy.
3. That blame, blame games and blame-avoidance, though they almost invariably get a bad press, are not all bad and that in some cases at least they can have positive effects on some conventional criteria for good governance.

If it is indeed possible to tell 'good' from 'bad' blame-avoidance, as has been suggested here, the problem then becomes that of how to encourage the positive kinds of blame-avoidance and discourage the negative ones. Some of the negative variants of the blame-avoidance strategies discussed here may be amenable to formal remedies (by Acts of Parliament, formal rules or what some legal scholars call 'soft law'). But many of those negative kinds of behaviour do not lend themselves easily to such remedies, because the harms they impose are subtle and often hard to define, and it is difficult to prohibit the negative forms of behaviour involved without over-inclusivity (that is, prohibiting forms of behaviour that should be allowed). If there are indeed limits to the extent to which we can discourage the wrong sorts of blame-avoidance by such legalistic, bureaucratic and technocratic means, the remedy must lie mainly in political processes. And that means politics with a small 'p' as well as a large 'P', in the sense of social processes of naming, shaming and claiming at every level from office politics to broader popular campaigns. In other words, if there are fixes for the blame-avoidance problem, those fixes must largely come from political and democratic pressures rather than from bureaucratic and technocratic routines.

References

Bentham, J. (1983) *Constitutional Code.* Oxford: Clarendon Press.

Better Government Initiative (2010) *Good Government: Reforming Parliament and the Executive.* London: Institute for Government and Better Goverment Initiative, www.bettergovernmentinitiative.co.uk/sitedata/Misc/Good-government-17-October.pdf (accessed May 2010).

Black, J. (2005) 'The emergence of risk-based regulation and the new public management in the UK', *Public Law* (autumn): 512–49.

Borraz, O. (2007) *Les politiques du risque: mémoire pour l'habilitation à diriger des recherches en science politique soutenue le 31 janvier 2007.* Paris: Sciences-Po.

Boyne, G. A., James, O., John, P. and Petrovsky, N. (2010) 'Does public service performance affect top management turnover?' *Journal of Public Administration Research and Theory* 20: 261–79.

Butler, D., Adonis, A. and Travers, T. (1994) *Failure in British Government: The Politics of the Poll Tax.* Oxford University Press.

Coser, L. (1956) *The Functions of Social Conflict.* London: Routledge & Kegan Paul.

Douglas, M. (1990) 'Risk as a forensic resource', *Daedalus* (Proceedings of the American Academy of Arts and Sciences) 119 (4): 1–16.

Duke Law Journal (1971) 'The medical malpractice threat: a study of defensive medicine', *Duke Law Journal* 5: 939–93.

Dunleavy, P. J. and White, A. (2010) *Making and Breaking Whitehall Departments: A Guide to Machinery of Government Changes.* London: Institute for Government/LSE Public Policy Group.

Flynn, P. (1999) *Dragons Led by Poodles: The Inside Story of a New Labour Stitch-up.* London: Politico's.

Hayek, F. A. von. (1978) 'Competition as a discovery procedure', in *New Studies in Philosophy, Politics and Economics*, pp. 179–90. Chicago University Press.

Heath, C., Larrick, R. and Wu, G. (1999) 'Goals as reference points', *Cognitive Psychology* 38: 79–109.

Hood, C. (2002) 'The risk game and the blame game', *Government and Opposition* 37: 15–37.

Hood, C. and Dixon, R. (2010) 'The political payoff from performance target systems: no-brainer or no-gainer?' *Journal of Public Administration Research and Theory* 20 (suppl. 2): 281–98.

Hood, C., Rothstein, H. and Baldwin, R. (2001) *The Government of Risk: Understanding Risk Regulation Regimes.* Oxford University Press.

Hood, C., Jennings, W., Dixon, R., Hogwood, B. W. with Beeston, C. (2009) 'Testing times: exploring staged responses and the impact of blame management strategies in two exam fiasco cases', *European Journal of Political Research* 48: 695–722.

James, O. and John, P. (2007) 'Public management performance information and electoral support for incumbent English local governments', *Journal of Public Administration Research and Theory* 17: 567–80.

Kahneman, D. and Tversky, A. (1979) 'Prospect theory: an analysis of decision under risk', *Econometrica* 47 (2): 263–91.

Kurtz, H. (1998) *Spin Cycle: Inside the Clinton Propaganda Machine.* New York: Free Press.

Lindbom, A. (2007) 'Obfuscating retrenchment: Swedish welfare policy in the 1990s', *Journal of Public Policy* 27: 129–50.

McCubbins, M. D. and Schwartz, T. (1984) 'Congressional oversight overlooked: police patrols versus fire alarms', *American Journal of Political Science* 28: 165–79.

McGraw, K. M. (1990) 'Avoiding blame: an experimental investigation of political excuses and justifications', *British Journal of Political Science* 20: 119–42.

Machiavelli, N. (1961) *The Prince*, tr. G. Bull. Harmondsworth: Penguin.

NERA (National Economic Research Associates) (2000) *Safety Regulations and Standards for European Railways.* London: NERA.

Pollitt, C. (1984) *Manipulating the Machine: Changing the Pattern of Ministerial Departments 1960–83.* London: Allen & Unwin.

Prat, A. (2005) 'The wrong kind of transparency', *American Economic Review* 95: 862–77.

Sulitzeanu-Kenan, R. (2006) 'If they get it right: an experimental test of the effects of UK public inquiries' appointment and reports', *Public Administration* 84: 623–53.

Sulitzeanu-Kenan, R. and Hood, C. (2005) 'Blame-avoidance with adjectives: motivation, opportunity, activity and outcome', paper presented to the European Consortium for Political Research joint sessions, Granada, April 2005.

Weaver, R. K. (1988) *Automatic Government: The Politics of Indexation.* Washington, DC: Brookings.

Weaver, R. K. (1986) 'The politics of blame avoidance', *Journal of Public Policy* 6: 371–98.

Further reading

Anheier, H. K. (ed.) (1999) *When Things Go Wrong: Organizational Failures and Breakdowns.* London: Sage.

Ellis, R. (1994) *Presidential Lightning Rods: The Politics of Blame Avoidance.* University Press of Kansas.

Felstiner, W. L. F., Abel, R. L. and Sarat, A. (1980) 'The emergence and transformation of disputes: naming, blaming, claiming', *Law and Society Review* 15 (3–4): 631–54.

Hood, C. (2011) *The Blame Game: Spin, Bureaucracy and Self-preservation in Government.* Princeton University Press.

Hood, C. (2002) 'The risk game and the blame game', *Government and Opposition* 37: 15–37.

Hood, C., Rothstein, H. and Baldwin, R. (2001) *The Government of Risk: Understanding Risk Regulation Regimes.* Oxford University Press.

Kurtz, H. (1998) *Spin Cycle: Inside the Clinton Propaganda Machine.* New York: Free Press.

Pierson, P. (1994) *Dismantling the Welfare State?* Cambridge University Press.

Power, M. K. (2007) *Organized Uncertainty: Designing a World of Risk Management.* Oxford University Press.

Weaver, R. K. (1986) 'The politics of blame avoidance', *Journal of Public Policy* 6: 371–98.

5 Risk and the humanities

Alea iacta est

MARY BEARD

Introduction

In a series of paintings from the walls of a bar in Pompeii – painted sometime in the ten years before Vesuvius erupted in AD 79 – is a scene of two Roman men playing a game of chance (Figure 5.1). They have a board between them balanced on their knees, and we can just about make out some counters on it. The man on the left has just been shaking the dice in a shaker, and, in the 'speech bubble' above his head, he is claiming a winning throw. 'I've won', he shouts ('Exsi' in Latin). 'No', says his partner and opponent, 'it's not a three, it's a two' ('Non tria, duas est').

The other paintings in the series show other activities you might expect to find going on in a bar: drinking, brawling, sex and flirtation (Figure 5.2). In fact, it is a line-up of exactly the kind of things that Roman puritans (who saw an obvious connection between alcohol, sex and dice-games) were very keen on deploring. It is perhaps hardly surprising that in the next painting (and so in the final episode of this little visual narrative), the game is leading to blows. Although the panel is badly damaged, it is clear enough that the two men have left the table and are trading insults in some almost incomprehensible speech bubbles. What we *can* understand is predictably rude: 'Look here cock-sucker (*fellator*) I was the winner.' Almost completely lost is the figure of the long-suffering landlord (or alternatively the hard-nosed supremo of the gambling den, depending on how we choose to see him). But his speech bubble survives. He is saying, as landlords have said for thousands of years: 'If you want to fight, get outside' ('itis foras rixsatis').[1]

[1] Clarke 2007: 120–5.

FIGURE 5.1 A game of dice from the painting on the wall of the 'Inn of Salvius' in Pompeii (now in the National Archaeological Museum, Naples). First century AD.

The scene is both familiar *and* deeply unfamiliar to us. It is familiar because we too are used to making that association between sex, violence, seedy drinking dens and the throw of the dice. But there is a much less familiar world here of danger, chance, uncertainty and what we (but not they) would call 'risk', whose principles I want to explore. No gamblers in ancient Rome, whatever their rough and ready common sense, would have formally conceptualised the idea that a six-sided dice had an equal, one in six, chance of landing on each of its six sides (perhaps, of course, given the irregularity of many ancient dice, they did not). And of course, when this pair left the bar and saw their local mountain puffing out smoke, they certainly did not engage in our kind of calculations of disaster planning; they might not even have sniffed risk or danger at all.

I am concerned with how men and women in the ancient world (and it is mostly men, I must confess) saw, represented and understood the uncertainties and dangers of their lives. I am also interested in what they

FIGURE 5.2 The full series of paintings from the 'Inn of Salvius' captures the story of life in a Roman bar – from a kiss, through more alcohol being provided by the waitress ('Whoever wants it, take it,' she says) to the final damaged scene of the quarrel – and the landlord's instruction to 'get outside'.

were anxious and uncertain *about,* which we should certainly not assume were the same issues as trouble us. I shall be concentrating on the world of the Roman empire from the first to the fourth centuries AD and I shall be trying, as far as I can, to look at the world of the 'ordinary' people rather than that of elite philosophers and their intellectual puzzles about luck, chance and divine providence. There is a notable tradition of ancient philosophical thought on this topic (in large part about how far luck can be a cause of anything, whether luck is different from chance, and whether luck or chance is 'automatic').[2] It is not, however, Plato, Aristotle or their Roman philosophical descendants, but the man in the street and in the bar, whose interests and fears I aim to recover.

This chapter is mainly an historical investigation. But I also want to ask if this ancient model of *danger* can still speak to us. When we reflect on how best to understand the dangers and risks of research and teaching in the humanities, might the ancient model I explore here actually be more useful than the current 'risk agenda' under which we are now asked to operate? That, at least, is the kite I fly at the end of this chapter.

Risk society: ancient and modern

Let us start by reflecting more carefully on some of the key differences between ancient (indeed any pre-modern) understanding and management of hazard and danger, and modern ideas of risk. Of course, modern definitions of risk themselves differ. There are debates and disagreements about how risk is to be managed or measured, even what it is to be called (is 'uncertainty', for example, a better term than 'risk'?). All the same, the simple fact that the 2010 Darwin lectures took *risk* as their theme was itself a nice illustration of how that idea occupies centre-stage in the contemporary academic and cultural agenda.

We can see the current resonance of risk in powerful, simple, albeit impressionistic, terms. Google News offers the opportunity of searching a wide range of international newspapers and magazines (those scanned

---

2 Classic passages are Aristotle, *Eudemian Ethics* 8, 2; *Physics* 2, 4–6 (where Aristotle considers whether a chance meeting with a friend in the market should really be ascribed to chance at all; no, he concludes, because the person had not gone to the market by chance but in order to buy something – which was therefore the cause of the meeting).

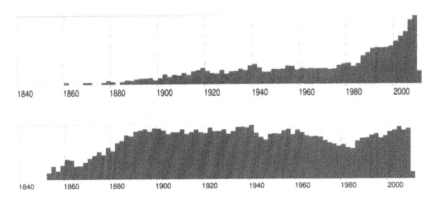

FIGURE 5.3 A snapshot of language change: the bar-chart shows the changing frequency of the word 'risk' in newspapers scanned by Google; the lower chart shows the frequency of the word 'danger'.

by Google). As Figure 5.3 shows, a search for the word 'risk' in the Google News archive reveals a dramatic, and recent, explosion. 'Risk' rarely occurs as a term in the news media until the end of the twentieth century, but an enormous take-off occurred in the early twenty-first century ('Christmas lights a serious safety risk', 'Women who walk reduce risk of stroke', 'How to reduce risk on Wall Street', and so on). This is not merely a reflection of the expansion of news media themselves, nor of Google's concentration on recent decades. For a comparable search for 'danger' shows no such change, but rather a more or less steady number of citations across the last two centuries (and so, in relative terms, a decline).

Google offers only a schematic glimpse. But it fits closely with the insistence of Ulrich Beck and Anthony Giddens that our own post-industrial society is a 'risk society'.[3] What characterises this 'risk society' are a number of key factors that we easily recognise in our own world and

---

[3] Beck 1992; Giddens 1990. Douglas and Wildavsky 1982 is a related discussion on cross-cultural ideas of risk and pollution.

behaviour: for example, our belief that relative degrees of hazard can in theory be estimated (even if in practice we may disagree on what the estimate is); and our belief that the state, and we as individuals, have a duty actively to manage risk and hazard (usually, in popular parlance, by avoiding it – though we also take 'calculated risks' when we choose, say, to go potholing or rock-climbing). Despite this, we can also feel powerless in the face of risk: for in an increasingly global world, the causes of hazard seem ever more outside our control. The classic case of this would be the fallout from the nuclear accident at Chernobyl, whose effects we could manage by not eating Welsh lamb, but whose causes were out of our power (it was something, like so many modern hazards, that *happened to us*, of which we were the victims). I shall, at the end of this chapter, suggest that modern universities have also come to see themselves as victims of hazard in a similar way.

The ultimate drivers behind modern risk society, why it developed when it did, are intensely debated. But everyone agrees that one necessary condition for being able to approach risk in this modern sense is what the philosopher Ian Hacking has termed the 'emergence of probability' – the development of the ability arithmetically to calculate chance.[4] In scientific legend, this goes back to 1654 when Pascal used probabilistic calculations to solve the problem of how to divide up the stake of an unfinished gambling game. True legend or not (and probably not), the date is roughly correct: probability theory (and the cognitive revolution that it launched) is a phenomenon of the seventeenth century.

In the Roman world, there are none of the key elements of our risk agenda. True the word 'probability' itself does derive from the Latin adjective *probabilis, probabile,* but in Latin that usually means 'worthy of approval' or 'commendable'; when it is used in a sense more like our own – that is, 'credible' or 'likely' – it is never associated with any form of calculation. The closest you come to that in Rome (and it is not very close) is in a discussion by the first-century orator, philosopher and wit, Cicero, of playing the knucklebones, which were an alternative form of dice made out of animal ankle bones, with four numbered sides. Cicero is talking about the so-called 'Venus throw' (the prized result, where each

---

[4] Hacking 1990 and 2006. See also (among many other discussions) Krüger, Daston and Heidelberger 1987.

of four knucklebones at a single throw displays a different number), and he draws a distinction between the chance of getting one Venus throw, and the chance of making 100 throws with every single one ending up a Venus throw. It is an argument that reveals some practical experience of dicing, but is a long way from a calculation of probability.[5] In this sense, to return to the dicers at Pompeii, arguing about a three or a two, they could not have seen those different outcomes in terms of probability in our sense.

As for the idea of responsibility for the management of risk, we need only reflect on the story of Egnatius Rufus, who, during the reign of the first emperor Augustus, at the very end of the first century BC, used his own slaves to act as Rome's first fire brigade. In our terms, it seems a classic instance of simple but sensible risk management. So was he honoured for the initiative? No, his actions were taken as a sign that he was currying favour with the people, and a sign that he was aiming at power and so a threat to the emperor himself. He was in due course found guilty of conspiracy and executed.[6]

How then do we deal with ancient approaches to uncertainty? One option is to try to discern some faint traces in the ancient world of a risk agenda not wholly dissimilar to our own, though much less explicit – and to re-create an 'embedded' discourse of risk within this apparently very different material. I shall examine one attempt to see rational risk management in Greco-Roman oracles in a later section of this chapter, exposing the problems with this method of approach.

For the most part, however, in the absence of anything like a calcula-tion of the probability of danger, let alone a recognisable risk agenda, we have tended to consign the ordinary Greeks and Romans to a world of unpredictable *dangers*. We have tended to see them as if they saw them-selves buffeted by the capricious whim of fate, or chance, or the gods – with little defence apart from keeping on the right side of the supernat-ural powers and hoping for the best, or shrugging their shoulders and

---

[5] Cicero, *On Divination* 1, 23; 2, 48 (the context of the discussion is whether one would need to see divine providence – Venus herself – behind the 100 Venus throws). Attempts – such as Garber and Zabell 1979 – to argue for some more finely conceptualised theory of probability in the ancient world have failed to prove their point.

[6] Dio Cassius, *History of Rome* 53, 24; Velleius Paterculus, *History of Rome* 2, 91–2.

Mary Beard

accepting that everything was pre-ordained anyway. That is maybe not wholly wrong (and certainly ancient philosophers were much engaged in the fine distinctions between chance, fate and divine providence). But I want to argue that there are clear signs of a much more positive engagement with ideas of uncertainty than that rather gloomy picture suggests.

If we are the inhabitants of 'risk society', the ancients – I want to argue – were the inhabitants of 'aleatory society'. This is a term that I am adapting from Nicholas Purcell's now classic study of Roman dicing (for which the Latin generic term was *alea*).[7] Purcell pointed to the analogy between success or failure with the dice and success or failure in other aspects of Roman life. Trade in particular, for the Romans, with all its hazards was a bit like a game of dice; it depended on luck – that is, it was *aleatory*. I want to push this further and to argue that it was not merely that various aspects of Roman life were *like* a game of dice (for that would not be far different from the passive model of danger I have just sketched), but rather that Romans used the imagery of dicing actively to parade (and so, in a sense, manage) uncertainty. They constructed other areas of hazard in their lives on the model of dicing, so that the luck of the board game became a way of seeing, classifying and understanding what in our terms might be thought of as risk. This was reinforced by a wider symbolic repertoire that I will not be able to discuss fully here but which included the personification of luck and good fortune as divine figures. One of the most famous, and much copied, statues of antiquity is the so-called 'Tyche of Antioch' – the 'luck' of the city of Antioch, in modern Turkey (Figure 5.4).

Dicing at Rome

Gaming with dice or knucklebones, often for cash, was an absolutely central activity across all ranks of Roman society, despite the emphasis in elite Roman literature on prohibition and regulation of the activity. Gambling is, for example, supposed to have been banned except on particular holidays, and Roman law limited the redress you could seek for

[7] Purcell 1995.

FIGURE 5.4 'The Tyche of Antioch' (the 'Luck' or the 'Goddess of Good
Fortune' of the city). She sits on a rock and at her feet the swimming figure
represents the River Orontes. The original statue was probably in bronze,
dating to *c*.300 BC. This is a plaster cast of one of the several surviving
versions of this popular work of art.

gambling debts.[8] Dice and knucklebones are found in huge numbers on archaeological sites, and gaming boards too survive in their thousands from the Roman world, in wood or more often scratched on stone: you can find them carved into steps in the forum at Rome, and a recent excavation of a Roman military camp on the Red Sea produced no fewer than twenty gaming boards, and possibly, or so the excavators boldly concluded, a special games room for playing.[9] The boards are of different forms and were clearly used for different games whose rules are now almost impossible to reconstruct (it is rather like trying to reconstruct the rules of *Monopoly* with just the board, some assorted houses and hotels and a 'Get out of Jail Free' card). But one of the most instantly recognisable boards seems to belong to an ancient type of backgammon, played with dice and counters, known as 'twelve-point' (*duodecim scripta*), with two or three rows of twelve squares or letters, serving as the points on to which to move the counters (Figure 5.5). Sometimes those letters are joined together into six-letter words, and then into sentences with a moral or ethical message ('PARTHI OCCISI BRITTO VICTUS LUDITE ROMANI', or 'The Parthians have been killed, the Briton conquered. Play on, Romans'; 'VENARI LAVARE LUDERE RIDERE OCCEST VIVERE', or 'Hunting, bathing, playing, laughing – that's living').[10] Morality and ethics were literally written into the game.

There are also thousands of ancient representations of games being played, or of dicing paraphernalia. An image from a different bar in Pompeii shows another gambling scene (Figure 5.6), as does a street scene in an elaborate mosaic from Roman Antioch (gaming tables can be seen in the open air, outside houses or shops).[11] They occur too on images from illustrated calendars, where the emblem of the month of December sometimes includes a dice and shaker (Figure 5.7) – an allusion to the fact that dicing was a major feature of the festival of Saturnalia, which took place in that month, and which is often seen as the ancestor of our

[8] The main ancient evidence is clearly laid out by Purcell 1995 and Toner 1995: 89–101.
[9] Still useful for the material remains (and one of the many attempts to reconstruct the rules) are Austin 1934 and 1935. The recent excavation is discussed by Mulvin and Sidebotham 2004.
[10] Purcell 1995: 19–28 discusses these and other examples.
[11] Megalopsychia Hunt Mosaic (fifth century AD) described and illustrated by Levi 1947: 326–37, plates LXXIX–LXXX.

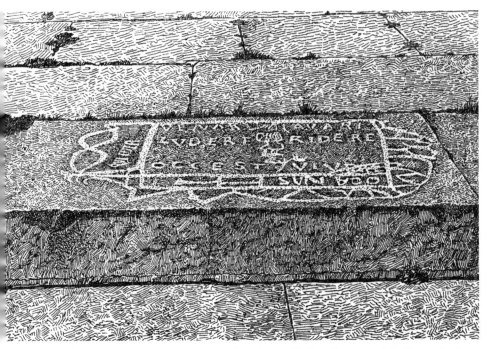

FIGURE 5.5 A gaming 'board', inscribed on the steps of the Forum in the Roman town of Timgad, in modern Algeria; you would presumably sit on the steps and pass the time with a game or two. Each of the letters (here making up the slogan 'VENARI LAVARE LUDERE RIDERE OCCEST VIVERE' – 'Hunting, bathing, playing, laughing – that's living') counted as a 'space' or 'square' on the board.

Christmas. We find them also on cheap pottery lamps and, predictably enough perhaps, on tombstones, where they stand not only for life's pleasures, but life's (and death's) lottery. There are even ancient verses, which describe tombstones decorated only with dice. One starts:

> This gravestone – come, let me see whose corpse it holds. But I spy
>
> No letter cut anywhere upon the stone.
>
> Merely nine thrown dice . . .

And it goes on to describe the throw shown by the dice on the memorial, which add up to cryptic clues about the dead man's name.[12]

---

[12] Antipater of Sidon (first century BC), from *Palatine Anthology* 7, 427, discussed by Goldhill 1994: 199–201.

Mary Beard

FIGURE 5.6 The gaming table, from the painting on the wall of the 'Bar on the Via di Mercurio' in Pompeii (still in situ). Two men sit at the table to play; two others stand to watch (and no doubt offer advice!). First century AD.

But the cultural importance of dicing runs even deeper than this might suggest, providing a way of 'modelling' the hazards of trade, politics and war, or even the construction of national identity. In his ethnography of the Germans, the Roman historian Tacitus insists that they *diced* differently from the Romans.[13] There is a striking political resonance too. One of the most familiar Latin quotes even now is the phrase 'alea iacta est' ('the die is cast') – the words that Julius Caesar is said to have spoken in 49 BC as he crossed the Rubicon to invade Italy and initiate that civil war which would lead to his own one-man rule over the city, and eventually to his assassination. There is some debate about the precise words used by Caesar. Our usual version derives from Suetonius' Latin biography of Caesar (though we tend to change the order of the words: Suetonius actually wrote 'iacta alea est'). The Greek biographer Plutarch, however,

[13] Tacitus, *Germania* 24.

96

FIGURE 5.7 The month of December from an illustrated calendar of the
fourth century AD (the so-called 'Calendar of 354'), shown here as in a
manuscript copy of the seventeenth century. A dice tower and two dice are
on the table beside the figure who personifies the month.

states explicitly that he shouted these words in Greek: 'ανερρίφθω κύβος'
('*anerriphtho kybos*'), which means literally '*let* the die be cast'; it was in
fact, as we learn elsewhere, a quotation from the fourth-century Greek
comic dramatist Menander.[14] In our own cultural repertoire the phrase
has become a slogan for 'the point of no return': as if Caesar was saying that civil war was now inevitable and there was no going back. But
that, surely, is to misinterpret what Caesar had in mind. By choosing the
metaphor of the dice, he was parading the uncertainty, the hazard and

---

[14] Suetonius, *Life of Julius Caesar* 60; Plutarch, *Life of Pompey* 60, *Life of Julius Cae-
sar* 32; Athenaeus, *Philosophers at Dinner* 13, 8 (Menander). Erasmus, the famous
Renaissance humanist, brought the two ancient versions into line by emending
Suetonius' 'est' to 'esto' – so making that phrase too mean '*let* the die be cast'.

the danger of the political and military outcome. The modern confusion may in part be connected with the traditional translation of the phrase: the noun 'die' is no longer a form currently in use as the singular of 'dice', but is still commonly used for the stamp or mould of a coin; the indelible stamping of a coin is an idea easily consistent with 'no turning back'.[15]

It should come as no surprise that dicing and gaming became an important element in the image of the emperors who followed Caesar. The emperor Claudius, for example, was said to be a dicing fanatic: he even wrote a book about it, and in a nasty Roman satire written shortly after his death he was envisaged languishing in the underworld and one of his peculiar punishments there was having to shake a dice in a bottomless dice-box, for eternity.[16] But dicing was also a means of displaying imperial power. The emperor Augustus was said to have been a keen dicer and gambler, so keen that he would provide his guests with their stakes to allow them to join him in an evening's gaming with no danger of leaving the party destitute. This is a nice illustration of the generosity of the emperor, but at the same time of his overweening power and control. For gambling ceases to be gambling if your host gives you the cash with which to do it. This is as close as we come to the display of the emperor's control over chance itself.[17]

In general, though, as this powerful and repeated insistence on dicing and its symbolism illustrates, Rome was a culture that looked danger in the eye. It did not attempt to avert or calculate danger, but rather to assert (almost celebrate) the uncertainties, chances and dangers of human existence. That is what I mean by referring to it as an *aleatory* society. This is a very different way of imaging danger from our own, but it is not exactly the passivity we sometimes project on to the Romans. They were not simply the dupes of Fate, they 'managed' danger by repeatedly reminding themselves to face it head on.

[15] I am very grateful to Michael Reeve for help on this point; though, as the citations in the *Oxford English Dictionary* make clear, the phrase is used to indicate 'the point of no return' from at least the seventeenth century (when 'die' was still common parlance as a singular of 'dice'). Purcell 1995: 26–7 raises further dicing and political implications of the ancient phrase.
[16] Suetonius, *Life of Claudius* 33; Seneca, *Pumpkinification of Claudius* 14.
[17] Suetonius, *Life of Augustus* 71.

Dice oracles

But there is even more to it than that. For, in fact, the throw of the dice could be used not only to expose uncertainty, but also to resolve it. I am thinking here of what are known as 'dice oracles' – a system whereby the numbers which came up on a throw of dice or knucklebones represented an answer to the question or problem troubling the thrower. This is nothing like the system of oracles found at the famous sanctuary of the god Apollo at Delphi, which has largely formed the modern popular image of ancient oracular practice. Here ancient kings and statesmen would come to consult the god and, so the stories go, they would leave with a riddling or ambiguous reply. In other words, the stock-in-trade of the oracular god at Delphi was to meet uncertainty with an almost equally uncertain response. So, for example, King Croesus of Lydia went to Delphi in the sixth century BC to find out if he should go to war against King Cyrus of Persia. The oracle said that if he did, he would destroy a great empire. Encouraged, he went to war, and he *did* end up destroying a great empire: the trouble was he lost and the great empire he destroyed was his own (the Delphic oracle had, perhaps, been hedging its bets).[18]

In fact, the vast majority of oracles in the ancient world (and by 'oracles' I am including everything down to street-corner fortune-tellers) were not riddling in this way. They gave a pretty clear steer, even if not absolutely straight answers, to their questioners. Some of these answers were, as at Delphi, authenticated as the voice of a god, but by no means all. Magic, arcane foreign lore, and the aleatory power of chance had a role too – as we see in dice oracles.

These were found widely, right through the ancient Mediterranean world, but they appear in a strikingly monumental form in some Roman cities in what is now Turkey, where large stone pillars were erected in the marketplace, inscribed with lists of all the fifty-six possible throws you can get with five knucklebones, and a response to match. Those responses were fairly standardised from one pillar to another, but not identical.[19] Consultation could not have been easier: you shook the knucklebones, looked up your throw on the pillar and found your answer.

---

[18] Herodotus, *Histories* 1, 53.   [19] Graf 2005.

So, for example, on the oracular inscription in the town of Kremna, put up in the first half of the second century AD by a pair of local benefactors, we read as one of the entries:

> 13344 15 Of Zeus the Saviour
>
> One Chian [i.e. a throw of one], two threes falling and the others are fours: the matter you undertake, be of good heart; go on, do it. Make the attempt. The gods displayed these oracles as favourable. Do not shun them in your intent; for nothing will harm you.

The predictions are not all so upbeat. On the gloomier side, a throw of 44444 gave the warning answer: 'Stop in the matters about which you ask me. For it is better neither to buy nor sell.'[20]

And so on.

These inscribed responses not only illustrate one important ancient use of dice, but they give us some access to what the men in the marketplace who used these oracles 2,000 years ago felt anxious or uncertain *about*. It is to this that I want to turn to now. For, while the parade of uncertainty and hazard is itself important, we also want to know what issues made people in the Roman world uncertain or anxious. For not every culture worries about the same things, or indeed worries most about what might seem to be its most pressing, its most 'real' dangers.

It turns out that these dice oracles are not perhaps as revealing in that respect as we might hope. Or rather they appear to be serving a niche market. For very many of the responses reflect anxiety about one area of life only, that is, business ventures, travel and trade. To quote the inscription from Kremna again: 'Hold back quietly from a journey away'; 'With regard to the road which you are going along, there is no profit from it for you.' True, they are not all concerned with business. There are a few responses that refer to illness or death ('The gods will save the sick man') and a number that offer rather unspecific predictions, both good and bad ('If you relax a little, you will achieve success'; 'Be on your guard!'). But where the reference is clear, it is mainly economic life that

[20] Horsley and Mitchell 2000: 22–8. In the entry for 13344, the second figure (as is standard throughout the text) gives the total that results from adding the previous five numbers together. Each throw is also associated with a god (Zeus the Saviour in this case).

is at stake. And, of course, that fits with the physical position of many of these oracular pillars: right in the middle of the commercial area of these little towns. It is as if these oracles simultaneously paraded the uncertainties of ancient commerce and offered a resolution to them.

The Oracles of Astrampsychus

An even more vivid glimpse of the varied anxieties of the Romans is provided by another set of oracular texts, several copies of which are preserved on papyrus. The introduction to these texts claims that they have been handed down from the mathematician Pythagoras, through the Egyptian magician Astrampsychus (hence their title, 'The Oracles of Astrampsychus'). They are even said to have been the favourite oracular devices of Alexander the Great, his secret decision-making process for conquering the world. In fact, all that is an entirely spurious, exotic advertisement (or celebrity endorsement) for what is probably a fortune-teller's handbook of, we guess, the second century AD.[21]

The system here is a more complicated one than that of the dice oracle. This was not a do-it-yourself method as the dice oracle probably was. The text we have was almost certainly one of the professional tools of the trade of a fortune-teller – and a good deal of obfuscation was built into getting an answer (presumably to protect the mystery, and the business, of the fortune-teller concerned). Let us begin by seeing how a consultation of the oracles would have looked to an outside observer, and then explore so far as we can the methods used by the fortune-teller and how our text played its part.

Imagine an 'anxious Roman' who needs an answer to his uncertainties. He goes to consult the fortune-teller, who hands him a numbered list of problems and asks him to choose from this list the number of the problem that most closely matches his concerns. (Presumably a good deal of impressive mumbo-jumbo accompanied even this first stage of the process.) The inquirer examines the list and chooses a problem: 'Number 100.' More mumbo-jumbo no doubt follows, and then the fortune-teller

[21] Two versions of the Greek text are available in two volumes of the Teubner series of classical texts: the first edited by Gerald M. Browne (1983), the second by Randall Stewart (2001). A composite version is translated in Hansen 1998: 291–324.

says (as magicians have said since time immemorial): 'Think of a number between one and ten.'

Now let's imagine that our inquirer chooses 'Number one'. Yet more mumbo-jumbo follows, until the fortune-teller reiterates: 'Tell me your number again.' Finally the fortune-teller beams (in this case) and says, 'I have good news for you, young man; for the oracles say "No, you will not get caught in adultery".' And off our anxious inquirer goes, happy.

It might not have turned out so well. If our inquirer had chosen the number six, the oracle's answer would have been 'You won't be caught as an adulterer *for the time being*', the number two would have produced, 'Yes you'll be caught in adultery soon', and the number seven would have brought a nasty surprise: 'You are not an adulterer but your wife is in love with someone else.'

So how was it done? And how did the written text that we still have produce an answer to the problems bothering the questioner? As we have just glimpsed, the consultation started from a list of ninety-two numbered questions that form the first part of the surviving text of the *Oracles*; these run confusingly from number 12 to 103 ('Will I be caught in adultery?', 'Will I inherit from my parents?' and so on). Our imaginary inquirer chose number 100 from the list ('Will I be caught in adultery?'). He then thought of his number between one and ten and the fortune-teller added that to the number of the question: 100 plus one equalled 101. The fortune-teller then went to another list (or 'Table of Correspondences'), also included in the text of the *Oracles*, which converted that total into a different number. According to the apparently random lists in the Tables of Correspondences the number 101 was converted into the number 32.

That still did not, by itself, produce the answer. But that new number would have directed the fortune-teller to one of a whole series of numbered groups of ten answers, or 'decades', which are the final part of the *Oracles*. For number 32 you went to decade 32, and within the decade that 'number you first thought of (in our case one) identified the particular answer that applied in this case: 'You won't be caught in adultery.' It was quite simple to operate – but if it *seems* baffling, that is exactly what it was meant to seem.

There are two important features here. First, each question posed had ten possible answers, and this takes us straight back to issues of the calculation of probability (or its absence) in antiquity that I have already mentioned. In an important recent book, Jerry Toner discerned some strikingly accurate probabilistic or – perhaps better – actuarial statistics embedded in this range of answers.[22] He looked, for example, at the ten possible answers that could be given in the *Oracles* to the question 'Will I rear the baby?' Three answers suggest that the baby will survive, three that it will survive with difficulty, two that it will die, one that it will be 'not reared' (a euphemism for exposed or killed) and one that it will thrive. Toner points out that this is not far from what we know of the demographic probabilities of an infant's survival in the Roman world (in which three out of ten would have died within the first year). And he went so far as to suggest that this oracular system was popular precisely because it reflected what we would call the *real* risks of the situation.

If that were true, it would be significant indeed (and indeed would undermine much of the modern history of probability); but it is probably not true. If some distributions of answers produce a 'realistic' probability, even more do not. Take for example the question: 'Am I being poisoned?', where four out of ten answers say 'Yes'. You might argue that anyone taking the trouble to ask whether they had been poisoned had a greater than average chance to be in an 'at risk' group, but even so, four out of ten seems in our terms to rate the risks rather high. Likewise, the eight out of ten positive responses to the question 'Will I become a town-councillor?' might indicate a relatively up-market clientele for the *Oracles* in general, or for this question a self-selected group of questioners (who only consulted the *Oracles* if they had a good chance of being elected anyway). Or it might indicate that there is much less connection between these oracular responses and social reality than Toner would like to imagine.

More interesting, as Toner himself would agree, is the range of uncertainties that these ninety-two questions reveal, where we see both anxieties that overlap with our own and a world of worry that is significantly different from ours. Similar is a whole array of questions about marriage, love affairs, sex, illness and commercial and career success: 'Is my wife having a baby?' (a question which has ten out of ten answers 'yes',

[22] Toner 2009: 46–52. A more general risk-based approach underlies Eidinow 2007.

either firmly scotching the actuarial line, or suggesting an unusual level of fecundity among the questioners); 'Will I get the girl I want?' (seven 'yes's, three 'no's, though at least one of the 'yes's says that you will get her, but then go off her), and one later Christian version of the text has 'Will I become a bishop?' (five 'yes's and five 'no's).

More striking, though, is the range of worries that do not match our own. I have already mentioned the question 'Have I been poisoned?' It is also clear that there must have been slaves among the inquirers, because 'Will I be sold?' is one question (giving us a tiny glimpse into slaves' uncertainties about their own future). But one significant surprise is the range of questions that refer to Roman law: 'Am I safe from prosecution?' 'Will I be informed against?' 'Will I argue my case?' We are used to thinking of the Roman legal system as a safeguard against danger, a protection for the citizen – or, in our terms, as a way of managing risk. That is not how it appears in the *Oracles of Astrampsychus*, where it is a menace, a threat and its processes are themselves something to be feared. This is a pattern of assumptions that fits with some of the technical terminology of Roman law, which actually overlaps with that of gambling. So, for example, the Latin word for the deposit that you put down on entering into a court case (or the agreement to pay a stipulated sum if the case was lost) is the same as one of the words for bet: *sponsio*.

To put it another way, we come back here to that story of Egnatius Rufus and his fire brigade. In the Roman world, some aspects of what *we* think of as the mechanisms of risk-aversion are seen as dangers in themselves.

Coda: risk, danger and the modern university

So does this world have anything to say to us when we think of risk in the modern university, and more precisely of risk in the humanities? I want finally to suggest, in a slightly devious way, that it does.

Anyone who has worked in our university system over the last twenty years can hardly have failed to notice how the risk agenda has encroached on much of what we do. If someone had told me when I first started teaching that I would end up filling out a risk-assessment form to take a group of ten young adult students on a sedate visit to the British Museum,

I would have thought they were joking. This is now what I do with only a slight sigh of irritation.

But some of this is more than irritating. It is hard not to be worried by what we might call the 'Chernobyl effect' in higher education's attitude to risk: the idea that risk comes free of responsibility for that risk. In going through the online risk assessments of (for the most part) American universities, it is hard not to be appalled. Among the *risks* you regularly find on these lists is 'quality of academic staff'. This is not just laughable, but it implies a truly 'irresponsible' view of university teachers and researchers on the part of their administration – as if they were a risk to be managed, not a group of people to be cherished, enhanced and supported, and as if it was not the duty of any university actively to ensure the high quality of its academic (and other) staff.

We see much the same thing closer to home in our own, changing, obsession with student plagiarism, which is also increasingly seen not as cheating, for which the student is responsible, but an appalling catastrophic ill that might just happen to the student, unawares. One of the best (or the worst) illustrations of this is the online anti-plagiarism quiz sponsored by the University of East Anglia: 'Are you at risk of plagiarism?' it is headed (which does not mean, as you might have thought, are you at risk of *being* plagiarised, but are you at risk of plagiarising).[23] There are thirteen questions aimed to get across such key facts as that 'plagiarism can happen accidentally, and you might not always know you have done it', that fear of plagiarism 'should not mean you don't talk to your friends about your work . . . ', and so on. It all makes plagiarism appear a bit like a nasty illness that you might contract without knowing it, but one that shouldn't prevent normal human contact (it might almost say – 'just don't share a toothbrush'). In fact, as one of my colleagues pointed out to me, 'plagiarism' *sounds* like an illness, 'cheating' does not.

But closest to my heart is the increasingly risk-averse agenda of humanities research, whether at doctoral level or in senior research projects. Twenty-five years ago in a completely different world, potential PhD students applied for 'British Academy grants', as they then were, by simply writing down a broad field of study, such as 'Roman History', 'English

[23] www.uea.ac.uk/menu/admin/dos/quiz/ (accessed 25 July 2010).

Literature', or whatever. Now our students have to write a whole essay, summarising their conclusions before they have even done the work. And any more senior scholar who has ever applied for AHRC (Arts and Humanities Research Council) research money will know all too well that you have to specify what the outcomes will be and even the timetable, week by week, towards achieving them. The AHRC has become so risk-averse in its selection procedures that the only safe and sensible way to get money out of them is to apply for funding for work you have actually already done. You then know the outcomes, can give a realistic timetable, and can use the research money to embark on another, new project.

We have come to think of all these mechanisms as prudence, and as the responsible management of public money. We seem to have forgotten that this is not how research in the humanities is carried out, certainly not good research. You do not know what you are going to find when you open a book, and you cannot say how long you will take to read it (it depends how interesting you make it). And an awful lot of the best work depends on a very great deal of *luck*. Indeed what distinguishes the successful humanities researcher from the less successful is, in part at least, that they are *lucky* – not that they have better managed the risks.

And this, of course, is where the Romans come in. Libraries are very *dangerous* places, and we should parade and face that danger. Research in the humanities is part of an aleatory culture, not a risk-managed culture. It is simply dishonest to pretend otherwise. *Alea iacta est* should be the motto of humanities research.[24]

References

Austin, R. G. (1934) 'Roman board games I', *Greece and Rome* 4: 24–34.
Austin, R. G. (1935) 'Roman board games II', *Greece and Rome* 4: 76–82.
Beck, U. (1992) *Risk Society: Towards a New Modernity.* London: Sage.
Bœswillwald, E., Cagnat, R. and Balla, A. (1905) *Une cité africaine sous l'empire romain.* Paris: E. Leroux.

[24] I have many people to thank for fruitful discussion in the course of preparing and writing up this lecture, especially: Christopher Kelly, Michael Reeve, Malcolm Schofield, Michael Scott and Jerry Toner. Thanks are also due to the Master, Fellows and students of Darwin College for trusting me with the topic and making the lecture series so enjoyable.

Clarke, J. R. (2007) *Looking at Laughter: Humor, Power and Transgression in Roman Visual Culture, 100 BC – AD 250*. Berkeley etc: University of California Press.

Douglas, M. and Wildavsky, A. (1982) *Risk and Culture: An Essay on the Selection of Technological and Environmental Dangers*. Berkeley, etc.: University of California Press.

Eidinow, E. (2007) *Oracles, Curses and Risk among the Ancient Greeks*. Oxford University Press.

Garber, D. and Zabell, S. (1979) 'On the emergence of probability', *Archive for the History of Exact Science* 21: 33–53.

Giddens, A. (1990) *The Consequences of Modernity*. Cambridge: Polity Press.

Goldhill, S. (1994) 'The naïve and knowing eye: ecphrasis and the culture of viewing in the Hellenistic world', in *Art and Text in Ancient Greek Culture*, ed. S. Goldhill and R. Osborne, pp. 197–223. Cambridge University Press.

Graf, F. (2005) 'Rolling the dice for an answer', in *Mantike: Studies in Ancient Divination*, ed. S. Iles-Johnston and P. T. Struck, pp. 51–97. Leiden: Brill.

Hacking, I. (2006) *The Emergence of Probability: A Philosophical Study of Early Ideas about Probability, Induction and Statistical Inference*, 2nd edition. Cambridge University Press.

Hacking, I. (1990) *The Taming of Chance*. Cambridge University Press.

Hansen, W. F. (ed.) (1998) *Anthology of Ancient Greek Popular Literature*. Bloomington: Indiana University Press.

Horsley, G. H. R. and Mitchell, S. (2000) *The Inscriptions of Central Pisidia: Including Texts from Kremna etc.* Bonn: Habelt.

Krüger, L., Daston, L. J. and Heidelberger, M. (eds.) (1987) *The Probabilistic Revolution*. 2 vols. Cambridge, Mass: MIT Press.

Levi, D. (1947) *Antioch Mosaic Pavements*. 2 vols. Princeton University Press.

Mulvin, L. and Sidebotham, S. E. (2004) 'Roman game boards from Abu Sha'ar (Red Sea Coast, Egypt)', *Antiquity* 78: 602–17.

Purcell, N. (1995) 'Literate games: Roman urban society and the game of *alea*', *Past and Present* 147: 3–37.

Strzygowski, J. (ed.) (1888) *Die Calenderbilder des Chronographien vom Jahre 354*. (Berlin: Drack und Verlag von Georg Reimer).

Toner, J. P. (1995) *Leisure and Ancient Rome*. Cambridge: Polity Press.

Toner, J. P. (2009) *Popular Culture in Ancient Rome*. Cambridge: Polity Press.

Further reading

The original Greek texts of the Oracles of Astrampsychus are available in:

Browne, G. (ed.) (1983) *Sortes Astrampsychi, volumen 1. Ecdosis prior.* Leipzig: Teubner.
Stewart, R. (ed.) (2001) *Sortes Astrampsychi, volumen 2. Ecdosis altera* Munich: Saur.

A translation is given in:

Hansen, W. F. (ed.) (1998) *Anthology of Ancient Greek Popular Literature.* Bloomington, IN: Indiana University Press.

ON ANCIENT ORACLES AND DIVINATION IN GENERAL

Eidinow, E. (2007) *Oracles, Curses and Risk among the Ancient Greeks.* Oxford University Press.
Iles-Johnston, S. (2008) *Ancient Greek Divination.* Chichester: Wiley-Blackwell.
Iles-Johnston, S. and Struck, P. T. (eds.) (2005) *Mantike: Studies in Ancient Divination.* Leiden: Brill.
Toner, J. P. (2009) *Popular Culture in Ancient Rome.* Cambridge: Polity Press.

ON ANCIENT GAMBLING

Purcell, N. (1995) 'Literate games: Roman urban society and the game of *alea*', *Past and Present* 147: 3–37
Toner, J. P. (1995) *Leisure and Ancient Rome.* Cambridge: Polity Press.

ON OTHER ASPECTS OF ANCIENT 'RISK'

Halstead, P. and O'Shea, J. (eds.) (1989) *Bad Year Economics: Cultural Responses to Risk and Uncertainty.* Cambridge University Press.

ON THE HISTORY OF PROBABILITY

Hacking, I. (2006) *The Emergence of Probability: A Philosophical Study of Early Ideas about Probability, Induction and Statistical Inference*, 2nd edition. Cambridge University Press.

6 Terrorism and counterterrorism

What is at risk?

LUCIA ZEDNER

Social scientists tell us we live in a 'world risk society'. But what does this mean post 9/11? By any account the risk to our collective security and, no less importantly, our subjective sense of security, was altered radically by the tragic events of that day. Of course terrorism was far from unknown before 9/11, but it did not occupy the public imagination in the way it has done since. Risk commentators were quick to add terrorist threat to the catalogue of environmental, health and engineering risks, and natural catastrophes already said to characterise the world risk society. But the risks born of terrorism are very different from those posed by climate change and 'flu pandemics. If risk is to avoid becoming an undifferentiated amalgam of unnamed perils we need to think a little harder about what or who is at risk.

This is all the more important because seeking security from terrorism has the quality of a trump card. Play the security hand and countervailing interests, not least our civil liberties, lose out. Despite their rarity, acts of terrorism pose a risk of catastrophic harm that inclines us to accept whatever policies seem to offer some prospect of protection. Although counterterrorist measures may discriminate unfairly and erode civil liberties unwarrantedly, the urge to reduce risk prevails. Balancing liberty and security assumes a zero-sum game in which by eroding liberty we can reduce risk. In place of balancing we would do better to think about the whole range of risks associated with terrorism and consider how seeking to avert risk may have the effect of introducing new hazards. By focusing on the obvious risks – threats to life and property, and subjective insecurity or terror itself – we risk overlooking the fact that countering terrorism carries its own hazards: risks to political and economic life; risks to social cohesion, community and race relations; risks to rights (rights to freedom of speech, privacy and freedom of the person) and risks for the rule of law. Add to this the risk of marginalising and alienating those we target and we arrive at the paradoxical situation that counterterrorism policies may make further attack more, not less, likely. So we need to consider what risks are really at stake when we seek to counter terrorist risk.

Assessing terrorist risk – hard science or speculation?

Risk has its roots in the natural sciences, where it involves probabilistic calculations of the likelihood of hazards occurring. Scientific measurement of risk is much more plausible in respect of physical and natural phenomena than in respect of the risks posed by human activity. When it comes to terrorism the data are less reliable still, so it is questionable whether one can safely talk of risk in a technical sense at all. We can observe some major differences in the uses of risk in this field.

First, the natural sciences deal in 'hard' data that are generally more robust, calculable and amenable to testing than the 'soft' data on human behaviour. The validity of predictions about the risks of stresses on a road bridge or fallout from a nuclear plant are of a different order from those that apply to terrorist activity. Human behaviour is not so easily reducible to the numbers needed for scientific calculations of risk and this limits our ability to make reliable predictions. The comparative rarity of terrorist attacks limits the scope for calculations that rely upon data sets sufficiently large for statistical significance. Despite highly developed and expensive security operations, intelligence about terrorist networks and their operations is sparse and erratic. As one US national security analyst observed, 'there is no "standard distribution curve" of past events that can be used to predict the future' of a terrorist attack.[1] Poor information, the dangers in trying to obtain it, and secrecy surrounding the work of intelligence agencies all combine to make hard facts difficult to come by in this sphere and raise serious questions about what reliance should be placed on terrorist risk forecasts (Figure 6.1).

[1] Anthony Cordesman quoted in Cornall 2007: 61.

SECURITYSERVICE

MI5

Current UK Threat Level:

The current threat level from international terrorism for the UK is assessed as **SEVERE**

The threat level for Irish related terrorism is set separately for Northern Ireland and Great Britain. In Northern Ireland it is **SEVERE** and in Great Britain **SUBSTANTIAL.**

SEVERE means that a terrorist attack is highly likely; **SUBSTANTIAL** that an attack is a strong possibility.

FIGURE 6.1 The 2010 UK threat levels.

Secondly, assessing terrorist risk is largely based on the subjective professional judgement of psychiatrists, intelligence experts and policy analysts. These data are then put to use by security agents on the ground, filtering them through a further layer of professional expertise and judgement. The technical language of risk calculation conceals a less systematic process by which professional judgements, personal and organisational interests stack up on one another to produce a more precarious edifice than the claims of science might suggest. Even where information exists, the need to protect intelligence agents, their sources and informants severely restricts the public availability of data on security threats and limits our ability to scrutinise decisions made by them.

Thirdly, terrorist risks differ in that the risk subjects are adaptive: that is, would-be terrorists have powerful motives to evade being identified as risky by altering their names, appearance, patterns of behaviour and their associates in order to avoid being categorised as high risk. Terrorists do risky things, but even suicide bombers want to avoid detection to ensure their operations succeed. Indeed, for terrorist groups whose influence depends on their reputation for effectiveness, detection is costly in terms of reputation well beyond the failure of the foiled plot. In general, scientific risks are not adaptive in this way. They do not respond to profiling, try to conceal their risk factors, or evade assessment. Put simply, the earthquake is no more or less likely to occur or the volcano to erupt because we monitor earth tremors or seismic activity. By contrast, risky behaviours by humans are fluid, changing in a bid to outwit measures taken against them. Managing the threat they pose requires strategies capable of responding to their adaptations and evasions. Hardening one set of targets against attack (for example by introducing metal-detectors at airport check-in) is liable to see terrorists changing tactics to evade screening (by using liquids rather than metal); by switching targets (the London underground rather than Heathrow airport); or elude profiling (using women or white men or Western names such as Anne Mary Murphy or Richard Reid). Such people fit no profile and come up on no airline screening list. Alter the profiles and terrorists respond so as to render precautions impotent almost as soon as they are made.

Fourthly, while no sphere of public policy is immune from politics, countering terrorism is a particularly hot potato. Recognising the highly charged political context in which risk-based strategies are implemented is important. The premium on public protection, the high level of interest and intense media coverage politicise terrorist risks to a degree unknown in most scientific spheres and distort both estimates of risk and responses to them. We will have more to say about this in due course.

Primary risks posed by the 'new terrorism'

Let us examine the primary risks posed by terrorism itself. Of course terrorism is not a new threat. The activities of the Irish Republican Army (IRA), Basque separatists (ETA) and the Red Army Faction (RAF) in Germany, among many others, have long posed a significant threat. Countries such as Israel, South Africa and Northern Ireland have lived with political violence for decades. What has changed is the sheer scale, fluid nature and global reach of the 'new terrorism', as it is known. The 2,823 people killed in a single day on 9/11 stands in striking comparison with the fact that since 1969 over the entire period of the 'Troubles' in Northern Ireland there was a total of 3,500 fatalities from terrorism. Not only is the scale of threat larger, but hidden: diffuse networks developed by al-Qaeda, stretching across an estimated sixty-five countries, make it very difficult to assess the risks posed by its members and affiliates. Intelligence about the nature and composition of these networks is likewise scarce and less easily reduced to suspect categories.

Whereas most prior terrorist organisations had identifiable hierarchies and known leaders, relatively transparent command structures and, in the case of the IRA at least, gave 'official' warnings before placing bombs against civilian targets, the rules of the terrorist game have now changed. The new terrorists resort to endlessly innovative (and hence inherently unpredictable) tactics and are willing to sacrifice their operatives as suicide bombers. In place of defined political goals the new terrorists subscribe to a potent religious creed of jihad in which every infidel is a target. Although al-Qaeda is often described as a network, it might better be thought of as a powerful ideology that excites emulation, with the result that quite unaffiliated individuals plan and perpetrate attacks in its name. Both the Madrid and London bombings were carried out by people inspired, but not directed, by al-Qaeda. These so-called 'lone wolves' are more difficult to detect: they are neither known to intelligence agencies nor do they fit existing profiles for terrorist suspects. Together these new features render the threats they pose both palpably greater and more difficult to predict.

That said, it is helpful to put what we do know about the statistical risks of terrorism in context. The facts are thought-provoking. For example, Mueller tells us that: 'An American's chance of being killed in one non-stop airline flight is about 1 in 13 million (even taking 9/11 into account), while to reach that same level of risk when driving on America's safest roads, rural interstate highways, one would have to travel a mere 11.2 miles.'[2] If one leaves out the fatalities of 9/11, fewer people have died in America from international terrorism than have drowned in toilets. Even if one includes the fatalities of 9/11, the number of Americans killed by terrorism since the late 1960s (when State Department records began) is about the same number as those killed over the same period by being struck by lightning or accident-causing deer or from a severe allergic

---

[2] Mueller 2005.

reaction to peanuts. In almost every year since records began, the total number of people worldwide killed by international terrorism is not much more than those who drowned in the bath. Until 9/11 the largest number ever killed in a single terrorist attack was 329 in an explosion on an Air India plane in 1985. Over the entire twentieth century, fewer than twenty terrorist attacks resulted in the deaths of more than 100 people.

By contrast, in the USA around 40,000 people per year are killed in road accidents.[3] Putting to one side for a moment the obvious reasons why 9/11 evoked such horror, let us address the more perplexing question of why deaths on the road do not excite our attention in the same way. Even in the UK (which has one of the lowest rates in Europe) deaths from road accidents are around 3,000 per annum.[4] To say that these deaths are tolerated may seem the ultimate in callousness. But the relative public acceptance of road traffic fatalities makes it difficult to conclude other than that raw magnitude alone is not decisive in determining which risks are deemed unacceptable and which are accepted as a fact of everyday life. Crucial perhaps is the malign intent behind every terrorist attack. As observed in this old proverb: '[E]ven a dog knows the difference between being stumbled over and being kicked.'

So a better point of comparison might be homicide rates. Again, the figures are interesting. For example, if one included the 2,823 people killed in the 9/11 attacks in the homicide figures for New York City that year, the city's official rate of 9 homicides per 100,000 population would have increased nearly fivefold to 44 per 100,000. Yet this rate is about the same as the homicide rates in cities such as New Orleans, Detroit and Washington DC, and much lower than the rate of 79 per 100,000 recorded in the city of Gary, Indiana.[5] This is not to downplay the tragedy that occurred on 9/11 – far from it – but to set it in context and to allow us to reflect upon how we respond differently to risks depending upon how and when they occur. Recognising that these very high annual homicide rates have not been thought to require exceptional measures or permit derogation from basic legal protections for suspects also invites us to consider whether the risks of terrorism should do so.

[3] Ibid.: 223 note 30.
[4] www.statistics.gov.uk/cci/nugget.asp?id=1208 (last accessed 1 July 2010).
[5] Rosenfeld 2004: 30.

Arguably, simply counting fatalities fails to take into account the larger financial, organisational and political costs entailed in terrorist attacks. The billions of pounds and hours spent on surveillance, screening and other security operations needs to be calculated in any attempt to quantify the costs involved. Estimating the true price of 9/11 is controversial and estimates vary widely, but reported figures suggest that the clean-up and stabilisation costs for the World Trade Center site were $9.0 billion; repairing and replacing damaged infrastructure $9.0 billion; rebuilding $6.7 billion; repairing and restoring other damaged buildings $5.3 billion; and the loss of rent $1.75 billion. In New York City, about 430,000 job-months and $2.8 billion in wages were lost in the three months following the attacks. Adding these costs to the shock, devastation and scale of the attack creates what we might call a 'catastrophe premium' that does not apply to deaths caused by road accident or homicide.

Rationality and risk

Arguably, numbers alone miss the important variable of human cognition: risks do not just exist 'out there' but are mediated through our perception and understanding in ways that alter their force and effect. To the concrete threats to person and property posed by terrorism, we need to add the subjective risks to our collective sense of security. Subjective security poses a real dilemma. How does one alert the public to security risks, encourage them to be vigilant (to the unattended bag for example) and yet carry on their lives as normal? A certain level of risk awareness serves to ensure that the population are prudent and willing to comply with security measures (particularly in arenas of higher risk like airports), but awareness risks hindering normal activity and causing us to limit our behaviour in ways that are counterproductive and costly to society. Counterterrorist measures and the political rhetoric used to justify them only serve to exacerbate public fear still further. Acknowledging public fear as a tangible harm serves to license extensions of state power, yet coercive measures impinge disproportionately on particular groups and minorities within society. Subjective security is important, but whether it should be permitted to license excessive liberty-eroding measures is doubtful.

The difficulty of minimising risks to subjective security is illuminated by research on the psychology of risk perception. A central problem is the disproportionate salience of the most publicised risks – what Tversky and Kahneman call the 'availability heuristic'.[6] If a risk occurs only rarely or is little known, we tend to underestimate its likelihood because we lack the ability to imagine its impact – it is not 'available' to us. When a risk does occur, it evokes shock and recrimination and in the wake of serious terrorist atrocities we tend to draw upon this tangible experience the better to understand our world and to anticipate the future. Lacking direct access to data that might enable us to calculate the statistical likelihood of further attack, we rely on readily available examples and, as a consequence, tend to overstate the risk of a similar catastrophic attack. So, for example, in the year after 9/11 many Americans took to the roads because they feared flying: an estimated 1,595 additional road deaths occurred as a consequence.[7] Notice also that the risks against which we demand protection are remarkably like the event that has just occurred: hence the focus on airport security and relative lack of concern about the security of ports or the Channel tunnel. Even security experts rely on the availability heuristic, for example when they focus on in-flight security post 9/11 or screen air passengers for liquids after a failed liquid bomb attack. Terrorists too are 'availability entrepreneurs'. They are masters at manipulating public opinion, distorting public perceptions, and generating fear of threats dislocated from the odds of them actually occurring. To maximise panic and disruption, threats issued by terrorists deliberately play on past experience and the difficulty we have in distinguishing between probability and impact.

Research on the psychology of risk reveals further factors that also distort perceptions. It appears we are overly impressed by the salience of unfamiliar and hard-to-control risks. Driving is high-risk but perceived as less risky than flying because we fly less frequently and cannot control our environment. We tolerate the relatively high risks inherent in driving because we have a sense of control (albeit probably false) over the risks we take, and because we value the convenience of cars. Uncertainty is

---

[6] Tversky and Kahneman 1974.   [7] Edwards 2009.

also a key factor. Apparently randomly distributed risks attract greater public unease, even if the incidence is low, because it is inherently difficult to assess whether we are at risk or not. Uncertainty makes it impossible to adapt behaviour or to avoid obviously 'risky' places or situations. Also important is the damage done to institutional trust, particularly when risks arise as a consequence of official incompetence. Where risks do not dent our trust in the officials or institutions we rely on for protection, our tolerance of them is higher than where public officials are implicated or our faith in government is undermined.

Our ability to estimate risks is further limited by what psychologists call 'probability neglect': that is, we have a tendency to ignore statistics, particularly if emotions are high.[8] We are more likely to focus on our fear of the bad outcome than upon statistical evidence as to the likelihood of it actually occurring. The enormity of a potential catastrophe blinds us as to evidence that it its likelihood is low. Media coverage amplifies and dramatises terrorist risks, distorting public perceptions further still. The result is that a fearful public irrationally demands governmental responses not warranted by the likelihood of the risk eventuating. Although this raises questions about the desirability of a populist politics in which citizens are over-demanding of protection, to regard the public as incapable of rational calculation might justify undue deference to expert knowledge. Deference is particularly hazardous given the likely extraordinary extensions of state power. How do we square the need for democratic accountability with evidence that the public, particularly a fearful public, is not well placed to make sound assessments of risk? Should we dismiss public fears as irrational or should we consider even the most distorted apprehension of risk as an independent harm worthy of government response? In resolving these difficult questions, public appreciation and tolerance of risk need to be taken into account alongside its scientific calculation. Subjective risk – the terror inherent in terrorism – is not reducible to technical measurement or statistical probability but is necessarily a matter of political decision-making and of public choice.

[8] Sunstein 2003.

Countering terrorism – a risky business?

So far we have considered the objective and subjective risks to our collective security posed by terrorism. But these are not the only risks in play. In what follows we turn to a different set of risks – the risks inherent in countering terrorism. The 9/11 attack and the 7/7 2005 London bombings significantly altered our political and legal landscape, launched the 'War on Terror' and, with it, a whole slew of new hazards that need to be factored into any analysis. Analysing the full range of risks entailed by the attempt to counter terrorism reveals it to be an inherently risky business. Let us consider a few of the more important risks in play.

First, *risk to expectations.* Even to talk of a War on Terror (capital W, capital T) raises public expectations unreasonably about what can be achieved. The war analogy implies that this is a campaign in which victory is possible, that the enemy can be defeated and an enduring peace secured. In reality the risk of terrorism from one source or another is probably ineradicable. We may introduce new legal powers, develop pre-emptive measures, and expend vast public funds in a bid to prevent it, but we can have no reasonable expectation of eliminating terrorist risks entirely. Criminologists have learned to talk about crime as a 'normal fact of everyday life'. Given the scale of the potential harms at stake, we can never hope nor should we try to think about terrorism with quite such equanimity. But acknowledging the enduring nature of terrorist risk might limit our ambitions, constrain the promises made and powers permitted to counter it. Greater realism might place a limit on coercive, liberty-eroding measures and encourage the general public to play its part by being vigilant and helping to minimise what we now recognise as constant risks. Better informing the public also reduces the danger that when we alter our behaviour to avoid feared risks we inadvertently generate new hazards born of those adaptations, as happened when Americans took to driving, rather than flying, after 9/11.

Being realistic about what protection can plausibly be promised is all the more important because quite another set of risks in play are the *reputational risks* faced by ministers, governments and public servants if attacks occur that call into question their professional judgement or expertise. The risk of getting it wrong in respect of catastrophic harms is potentially ruinous to political reputation and electoral support. Likewise, security and police chiefs stand to suffer devastating damage to their professional standing if they fail to foresee or pre-empt an attack, so they tend to be constitutionally risk-averse. Generally, underestimating a threat poses a far greater risk to reputation than overestimating it. Little blame attaches to the security chief who takes too cautious an approach, if no threat arises; whereas the security chief who ignores a warning or fails to take preventive measures will likely suffer huge reputational loss (or dismissal) if that risk eventuates. Of course overestimating and misattributing risks can also result in actions ruinous of reputation and tragic in their consequences. The shooting of an innocent man, Jean Charles de Menezes, on the London underground by the Metropolitan Police just weeks after the July 2005 London bombings and a day after a failed further bomb attack is an obvious example. In this case extreme caution resulted in a tragic loss of life that had major ramifications for the reputation of the Metropolitan Police and its Commissioner, who resigned as a consequence. So we need to add to our basket of risks political, professional and reputational risks as potential costs in countering terrorism and recognise that avoiding them can have the effect of distorting priorities and damaging decision-making.

Less obvious still are *organisational risks* to an institution's ability to function effectively. An important consideration in counterterrorism is the need to minimise risks to the efficacy of intelligence services and the police. Potential risks to the security of operations, agents and their informants act as a bar on disclosure of intelligence. Organisational risk here is said to justify security classifications that deny public access to information, excuse the use of redacted evidence, and allow the use of 'special advocates' (security-cleared lawyers) permitted to see evidence against their clients but not divulge it to them. Protecting the interests and operations of security organisations is privileged over the historic right of defendants to see the evidence against them. Note also that these same organisations have a vested interest in magnifying risks in order to secure greater power and resources. The larger the purported risk, the higher the funding, the stronger the legal powers and the bigger the role their organisation can claim.

These considerations partly explain the extraordinary and fast-growing resources allocated to security. Countering terrorism is an expensive business and we need to be alert to the *opportunity costs* entailed. In 2007 the UK Comprehensive Spending Review announced: 'security spending is planned to reach £3.5 billion by 2011. This includes an additional £240 million in funding for counter-terrorist policing and over £100 million to improve our ability to stop people becoming or supporting terrorists.'[9] This huge investment of public funds in security programmes clearly poses a hazard to other areas of government endeavour. The billions spent on security are not then available for the pursuit of other public goods such as education, health and welfare. Importantly, deploying opportunity costs as a check on government power can be expected to appeal across a broader political spectrum than the traditional, left-liberal defence of civil liberties.

Countervailing risks

Let us now turn to a rather different and even more alarming set of risks, namely the danger that counterterrorism policies spawn countervailing risks or new security threats. So-called *risk–risk tradeoffs* are a commonplace of the field and require risks to be weighed in a bid to determine which strategy or measure is most likely to reduce all the risks entailed and least likely to result in the perverse consequence of reducing one risk only to create another. Risk–risk tradeoffs are most acute in emergency or crisis situations. Tackling terrorist hostage-taking, for example, often results in the death of the hostages as well as the terrorists; while, as we have seen, arming airline personnel or the police can result in civilian deaths.

Beyond the hard choices thrown up by emergency situations, ongoing security policies may produce countervailing risks that are less immediate and obvious though no less grave. Security policies that target minority communities or particular classes of individual (for example young men of middle-eastern appearance) have a detrimental effect on their well-being, social life, levels of integration, and ability to move around the world unhindered. The effect of being targeted by security measures may foster a sense of isolation and alienation. Over time, counterterrorist policies

[9] Home Office 2009: 18.

may exacerbate the risk of resentment and hostility that predispose those so targeted to religious radicalisation or political extremism. Ironically this is conducive to their recruitment by terrorist groups.

It is by no means only domestic counterterrorist policies that have this effect. The invasion and occupation of Iraq is the best known instance of a policy justified on the grounds of counterterrorism that served to increase significantly new recruits to terrorism. Guantanamo, Abu Ghraib and the practice of rendition were similarly inflammatory in their effect, while publicity surrounding the torture, degrading treatment and humiliation of terrorist suspects may have recruited many to join terrorist cells. To give a fuller picture of these countervailing risks would require more systematic analysis of the effects of counterterrorism policies on the alienation and disaffection of those targeted.

Important too are *risks to wider community relations* and, not least, the relations that police and security services have with the very communities they rely upon for intelligence about possible future terrorist attacks. Practices such as profiling of terrorist suspects and dawn raids upon minority communities may entrench suspicion among the public at large. Even ostensibly neutral counterterrorist laws and policies, if applied in ways that in practice discriminate against particular religious or ethnic minority communities, have the effect of damaging intra-community relations, stirring up racial or religious hatred and are unjust. These risks to targeted communities or suspect populations are prime examples of how measures intended to counter terrorism can too easily generate new risks that need to be traded off against security gains. Precautionary measures that serve only to recruit terrorists, displace terrorist activity to softer targets, or achieve security in one sphere at the expense of another may turn out to increase rather than decrease risks overall, since we know that compliance with the law is highly dependent upon procedural justice and perceived legitimacy.

Collateral risks

In addition to risks to security we need to be alert to risks to the very institutions and values we seek to protect against the terrorist threat – not least liberal democracy and the rule of law. Much of the debate post

9/11 has focused on the priority of pursuing security, and the inevitability of forgoing civil liberties to this end. In times of crisis or emergency, it is argued, we should not be too precious about protecting civil liberties that stand in the way of measures capable of averting a terrorist attack. Surveillance, profiling, identity cards, DNA databases, extended powers of arrest and detention, and special procedures are just a few of the most obvious liberty-eroding measures. Yet these responses to the risk of terrorist attack generate new risks to human rights. Rights to freedom of speech, to privacy, to the presumption of innocence, to counsel, to a fair trial, and even to personal freedom are all casualties of this approach. Instead of setting up a problematic binary between security and liberty, in which liberty is always liable to lose out as a luxury we cannot afford when the stakes are high, we might do better to recognise the *risks to rights* posed by these counterterrorist measures.

Of course there are good reasons for permitting the state to authorise the use of coercion to protect the public from catastrophic harms. Preventive measures permit the police to intervene before harm occurs and the courts to incapacitate those who pose a danger to society. They may even have a deterrent effect upon prospective perpetrators (suicide bombers may be willing to risk death but not the failure of their enterprise). Yet powers to intervene early and in respect of actions remote from the commission of an attack carry the risk of rendering illegal conduct which would otherwise be lawful and of permitting premature and potentially oppressive or intrusive measures that erode individual liberties and pose a serious *risk to the rule of law*.

Recent years have witnessed a remarkable proliferation of counter-terrorism policies that alter the very nature of criminal liability. The scope of the criminal law has been extended under successive counter-terrorist laws that criminalise glorifying, encouraging, assisting, planning and preparing terrorist attacks, and publishing and disseminating terrorist literature. Given that the very definition of terrorism is wide enough to capture many forms of political protest and civil disobedience, the risks of over-criminalisation should not be ignored (Figure 6.2).

In addition, new legal forms are being developed. The most important is a novel species of hybrid or 'two-step' measure: the Control Order is brought in civil proceedings and imposes quasi house arrest and

Terrorism Act 2000 Section 1. Terrorism: interpretation

(1) In this Act 'terrorism' means the use or threat of action where:

(a) the action falls within subsection (2),

(b) the use or threat is designed to influence the government [or an international governmental organisation] or to intimidate the public or a section of the public, and

(c) the use or threat is made for the purpose of advancing a political, religious, racial or ideological cause.

(2) Action falls within this subsection if it:

(a) involves serious violence against a person,

(b) involves serious damage to property,

(c) endangers a person's life, other than that of the person committing the action,

(d) creates a serious risk to the health or safety of the public or a section of the public, or

(e) is designed seriously to interfere with or seriously to disrupt an electronic system.

FIGURE 6.2 Legal definition of terrorism

considerable restriction of movement and association on terrorist suspects when the Home Secretary 'considers that it is necessary, for purposes connected with protecting members of the public from a risk of terrorism'.[10] But despite being a civil order it is backed by lengthy imprisonment for breach, allowing the civil law to be used for criminal law purposes, but without the procedural protections normally provided to defendants. Not surprisingly, Control Orders have been subject to a long run of appeal cases questioning their compatibility with important human rights.[11]

Legal responses to risk need to be reconciled with fundamental principles such as certainty, transparency, proportionality and equality. Decision-making in fields like environmental risk or nuclear power only rarely has to grapple with the serious threats to civil liberties posed by security and counterterrorist policies. Where individual liberties are at stake the impulse to err on the side of precaution comes at a far greater cost. Recognising risks to rights and the rule of law makes it absolutely clear that more than one set of risks are in play.

[10] Prevention of Terrorism Act 2005 S.2(1)(b).

[11] In January 2011 the government announced their intention to replace Control Orders with 'terrorism prevention and investigation measures' or Tpims. These have been widely criticised as continuing the Control Order regime in all but name.

Who is to decide?

By now it should be clear that the risks posed by terrorism are many and varied. This raises the thorny question of who should assess and weigh these risks, not least in order to resolve what level of intervention and what measures are necessary and proportional. This involves important issues about the role of expert knowledge, political accountability and adherence to the rule of law. Should assessing the risk of terrorist attack be considered a matter of technocratic determination – best left to the intelligence agencies and risk experts? Or is it properly a matter of political deliberation and democratic engagement? Our answer might depend upon the nature of the particular risks to be forestalled. If objective risks to public safety are at issue this might place the onus on the experts (be they security agents, intelligence services or risk analysts). Given that, as we have shown, the public are liable to misperceive risk and overestimate their need for protection, it has been argued that assessment is better left to the experts. This assumes of course that we can have confidence in them, that their deliberations are unbiased, and that deference to their expertise does not diminish accountability.

On the other hand, if the primary risk to be averted is public fear, then public confidence in the ability of the state to protect becomes crucial. Fear need not point to a populist approach in which public opinion is simply allowed to dictate policy. A more sophisticated approach would allow expert opinion, political scrutiny and public debate to be brought to bear upon the twin activities of assessing and managing risk, in recognition of the fact that the issues at stake are not merely evidential or technical but political. How large must a risk be before we take costly steps to avert it? Where the statistical probability of attack is low, what level of spending and what erosion of civil liberties are merited? How do we measure the risks to other public goods (community, privacy, freedom of speech) and public projects (health care, education, social welfare) implied by security programmes? Is fear itself a cost that should weigh in the balance? Do risks to subjective safety suffice as a ground for security measures that are costly or detrimental to others' interests? If the public are irrationally fearful should the government respond? And, if so, how?

We have seen how populist responses to terrorism are liable to be skewed by strong emotions, the tendency to exaggerate risks and the distorting effects of seeking to avoid reputational, professional and organisational risks. Public fear and political considerations are legitimate concerns but they risk allowing terrorism to become a licence for a new terror – the terror of prevention – in which protecting the majority licenses oppressive measures that target selected groups. Yet if an overly populist response to terrorism has its perils, so too does undue deference to expert knowledge or technocratic expertise. Deference is problematic because intelligence experts may be less well equipped to assess and weigh the range of other collateral and countervailing risks discussed so far. Moreover, since much intelligence remains undisclosed to the public, deference here severely limits open political deliberation. It is probably inevitable, particularly in times of heightened security risk, that the executive will grant itself extraordinary law-making powers. But this is not to say that its exercise of those powers should remain beyond scrutiny.

The role of the courts here is crucial. Whereas Parliament may be directly pressured by public fear, the courts, at one step removed, are arguably better placed to question the need for new powers and to ensure that derogations are temporary, proportional and actually necessary. By virtue of their structural independence, judges are particularly well placed to scrutinise decisions concerning the most vulnerable and most excluded. In so doing, they also serve security in the less usual sense of securing the interests of individuals against the power of the state. As Feldman argues: 'The judiciary alone voluntarily shoulders the discipline of rationally and publicly justifying its decisions; the judiciary alone subjects itself to the further discipline of framing its justification by reference to legal norms and objective standards.'[12] Close and critical judicial scrutiny might well be backed by a culture of presumptive mistrust in which judges regard all new counterterrorist powers (especially those that burden selected subgroups disproportionately) as inherently suspect and in need of justification. The greater the risk to the civil liberties of the few, the heavier should be the burden of judicial scrutiny of the supposed justifications for new measures. Judicial scrutiny also has the advantage of taking place *ex*

[12] Feldman 2006.

post facto, identifying prior errors and overstated claims, and so improving the framework used for future decision-making. As such the judiciary has a vital role to play as a 'crucial institutional safeguard against policies motivated primarily by fear'.[13] That said, judicial oversight depends upon the courts having adequate access to the information and intelligence upon which executive decisions are based; where access is denied, judicial capacity to challenge and check the executive is necessarily diminished.

Surviving risk through resilience

Although it is neither possible to eliminate the risks of terrorism nor costless to try to do so, acknowledging its ineradicable quality need not entail passive resignation. An important counter-strategy is to be found in the notion of 'resilience', a term with distinctly Darwinian overtones. Resilience underscores the attempt to find ways of living with, minimising, and, importantly, surviving risk. Resilience strategies seek to identify areas of vulnerability, build resistance to threats and guarantee the critical infrastructure needed to ensure rapid recovery after catastrophic events. Put simply, resilience is the capacity to absorb shocks and bounce back.

The modern conception of resilience is very distant from the much-ridiculed UK 'Protect and Survive' campaign of the 1970s, which aimed to increase public preparedness for a nuclear attack, or the American campaign which invited the public to 'duck and cover' in case of nuclear warning. Today's resilience programmes entail sophisticated strategies, networks and measures that seek to tackle the entire portfolio of risks in play. Resilience strategies typically emphasise preparedness for emergencies, rapid response, recovery programmes and mitigation of loss. Brittle infrastructures, be they energy supplies, communication or transport systems, are very vulnerable to terrorist attack and are a focus of resilience programmes (Figure 6.3). So, for example, the British government's 'Contest Strategy' maintains that '[p]rotective security measures for transport systems must reduce the risk of attack, increase resilience to attack, have minimal disruptive impact and retain the confidence of people who are travelling'.[14]

---

[13] Ramraj 2005: 108.   [14] Home Office 2009: 107.

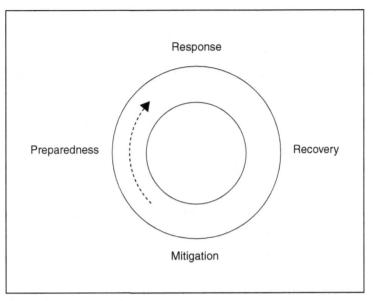

FIGURE 6.3 The social resilience cycle

Resilience is not a matter for central government alone. New security programmes seek to counter the risks to community cohesion and race relations. The UK National Security Strategy tries to increase the resilience of communities by strengthening civil society, enhancing economic opportunities, and providing education and training with the objective of reducing the risk of alienation and radicalisation. At a local level, new multi-agency partnerships, such as Regional Resilience Forums, are tasked with assessing risks in their areas and preparing and testing plans to tackle them. Other locally based initiatives include the Channel Project, which is a community-based multi-agency initiative to support vulnerable individuals using existing partnerships between the police, local authorities and communities. The project takes referrals of individuals considered susceptible to becoming involved in violent extremism and institutes programmes of intervention designed to avert this risk.[15] Other projects focus on tackling the risk of radicalisation in prisons and in the asylum system among the alienated youth detained there. Engaging, educating,

---

[15] Edwards 2009: 172.

empowering and encouraging communities are important means of ensuring resilience from the bottom up.

Resilience is sought not only through preventive strategies but also by ensuring that when a catastrophic risk does occur, individuals, communities and organisations have the capacity to bounce back. Here resilience entails ensuring the necessary resources, infrastructure and networks to tackle the effects of a terrorist attack and to minimise the harm, damage and disruption it causes, for example to medical and emergency services, to communication and transport networks. The aim is to limit impact, reduce consequent hazards, mitigate disruption to services, ensure continuity and so enable swift recovery. The lessons learned from 9/11 and the July 2005 terrorist bombings in London made clear the importance of preparedness. These include: 'providing better support to the bereaved and survivors, timely information to the public and more resilient telecommunications capabilities between responders'.[16] In the immediate aftermath of an attack the emphasis is on rapid distribution of clear and accurate information to alleviate public anxiety, help the public to protect themselves from further danger and inconvenience, assist emergency services and inform subsequent criminal investigations. In the longer term the focus shifts to ensuring that critical national infrastructure remains intact; that it continues to deliver essential services; and that disruption to social and political life and to the economy is minimised and the return to normality is expedited.

Conclusion

In other spheres of economic, social and political life academics encourage us to 'embrace risk' or to appreciate the 'uncertain promise of risk'.[17] The idea of embracing risk is hardly plausible in respect of terrorism, where taking risks promises little gain and failure to avert results in catastrophic harm. That said, since we cannot hope to eliminate the threat of terrorist attack entirely, we must learn to live with risk here as elsewhere. Not least because, as we have shown, there are far more risks at stake than the threatened attack. Trying to eliminate the risk of terrorism spawns

---

[16] Ibid.: 120.   [17] O'Malley 2004.

its own risks. Waging an all-out War on Terror would entail intolerable costs to political freedom, social cohesion, tolerance, diversity, human rights and other important attributes of liberal democracy under the rule of law. Systematic analysis of the full portfolio of potential risks in play can act as a powerful counterweight to demands for security measures or policies targeted only against the most obvious risks that terrorism poses. Undertaking a comprehensive review of all the risks, opportunity costs, collateral harms and countervailing risks is a surer way of enabling us to appreciate what really is in jeopardy when we demand security against terrorist risks and of ensuring critical oversight and scrutiny. Resilience strategies provide alternative means of reducing risk, lessening the impact of attack and enhancing our collective ability to pull through. Such strategies might just enable us to learn to live with risk without living in terror.

References

Cornall, R. (2007) 'The effectiveness of criminal laws on terrorism', in *Law and Liberty in the War on Terror*, ed. A. Lynch, E. Macdonald and G. Williams, pp. 59–74. Annandale, NSW: Federation Press.

Edwards, C. (2009) *Resilient Nation*. London: Demos. www.demos.co.uk/publications/resilientnation (last accessed 1 July 2010).

Feldman, D. (2006) 'Human rights, terrorism and risk: the role of politicians and judges', *Public Law*: 364–84.

Home Office (2009) *Pursue Prevent Protect Prepare: The United Kingdom's Strategy for Countering International Terrorism*. London: HMSO. tna.europarchive.org/20100419081706/http://security.homeoffice.gov.uk/news-publications/publication-search/contest/contest-strategy/contest-strategy-2009?view=Binary (last accessed 1 July 2010).

Mueller, J. (2005) 'Simplicity and spook: terrorism and the dynamics of threat exaggeration', *International Studies Perspectives* 6: 208–34.

O'Malley, P. (2004) 'The uncertain promise of risk', *Australian and New Zealand Journal of Criminology* 37 (3): 323–43.

Ramraj, V. V. (2005) 'Terrorism, risk perception and judicial review', in *Global Anti-Terrorism Law and Policy*, ed. V. V. Ramraj, M. Hor, and K. Roach, pp. 107–26. Cambridge: Cambridge University Press.

Rosenfeld, R. (2004) 'Terrorism and criminology', in *Terrorism and Counter-Terrorism: Criminological Perspectives*, pp. 19–32. Amsterdam: Elsevier.

Sunstein, C. R. (2003) 'Terrorism and probability neglect', *Journal of Risk and Uncertainty* 26: 121–36.

Tversky, A. and Kahneman, D. (1974) 'Judgment under uncertainty: Heuristics and biases'. *Science* 112: 61–117.

Further reading

Ackermann, B. (2006) *Before the Next Attack: Preserving Civil Liberties in an Age of Terrorism*. New Haven, CT: Yale University Press.

Cole, D. (2003) *Enemy Aliens: Double Standards and Constitutional Freedoms in the War on Terrorism*. New York: New Press.

Dershowitz, A. (2003) *Why Terrorism Works: Understanding the Threat, Responding to the Challenge*. New Haven, CT: Yale University Press.

Hewitt, S. (2008) *The British War on Terror: Terrorism and Counter-Terrorism on the Home Front since 9/11*. London: Continuum.

Ignatieff, M. (2004) *The Lesser Evil: Political Ethics in an Age of Terror*. Edinburgh University Press.

Lynch, A., MacDonald, E. and Williams, G. (eds.) (2007) *Law and Liberty in the War on Terror*. Annandale, NSW: Federation Press.

Posner, R. (2004) *Catastrophe: Risk and Response*. Oxford University Press.

Sunstein, C. (2004) *Laws of Fear*. Cambridge University Press.

7 Risk and natural catastrophes

The long view

MARK BAILEY

Summary

Natural catastrophes – rare, high-consequence events – present us with a unique conjunction of problems so far as risk is concerned. Firstly, they can have an extremely long recurrence interval – so long that the greatest may not have occurred within human memory. Secondly, the effects of events with which we are all too familiar, for example earthquakes, floods, volcanoes and storms, are easily trumped by the impacts of objects – comets and asteroids – that reach Earth from outer space; and thirdly, the largest of these events have a global reach, in principle threatening not just our way of life but perhaps life on Earth itself. However, recognising that such events occur very rarely, should we 'make hay while the sun shines' and ignore, ostrich-like, the significant actuarial risk; or should we seek to understand the underlying phenomena and develop strategies to mitigate the threat, and perhaps technologies to avert it? Our individual response often depends less on a purely rational assessment than on personal circumstances and how we have been brought up. In any case the nature of the risks, which are poorly understood, means that we must be prepared to handle the law of unintended consequences (that is, could our actions make things worse?). We must also be prepared to explore what happens if, perhaps inevitably, our current scientific understanding turns out to be less certain than many experts believe.

Introduction

Rare, high-consequence events present society with exceptional difficulties so far as risk assessment is concerned. The infrequency of the

131

most extreme events means that their causes are often among the most poorly understood among environmental issues and their impacts are – fortunately – poorly known from direct experience. In addition, natural catastrophes may have an origin either entirely within the Earth-system or from outside: from the Sun, solar system or wider Universe of which the Earth is a part. It is widely accepted that the potentially devastating effects of cosmic phenomena are likely, in the long term, to far outweigh any purely Earth-based cataclysm.

In this chapter, we first describe the canonical framework for risk assessment in the context of natural catastrophes and major societal events. There follows a broadening of the discussion to include the implications of natural disasters ultimately triggered by events occurring outside the Earth, in our solar system. These phenomena, coming at us from a source in outer space, exceed in terms of magnitude the worst possible hurricane or earthquake, and have the potential to cause very significant loss of life – even mass extinctions of species – and to change the course of evolution of life on our planet. The final part of the paper presents a more speculative aspect of this story, highlighting the fact that there are more uncertainties, even in astronomy, than many experts are generally prepared to acknowledge. This raises the uncomfortable question of the limits to knowledge and how these systematic unknowns can be best planned for.

The 'long view' of astronomy thus raises many questions for risk assessment, for how we perceive ourselves, and for our views on the development of society. For example, do we ignore rare, high-consequence hazards that have an extremely low probability of occurrence in our lifetime or even those of our children and grandchildren, palming, as it were, the responsibility for managing the risk on to successive generations? Similarly, how much should we in the developed world do in order to quantify and mitigate potential global hazards, when we have relatively few natural resources at our disposal and when our population is only a very small fraction of that of the whole world. In short, who should take care of global hazards: are they our responsibility because we recognise them, or does the ultimate responsibility fall to others, perhaps those more wealthy than ourselves or more at risk from the identified threats?

In dealing with these questions it is sometimes helpful to consider human life and civilisation as if it were an organism with a lifetime measured in thousands or perhaps millions of years. Would such a creature, with a memory of natural catastrophes occurring over long time-scales and with a life expectancy up to millions of years, respond differently to long-term risks than we currently do, whether as individuals, national governments or international organisations?

Finally, having identified a risk, for example – as in astronomy – by curiosity-driven research, how should we allocate the necessary resources to achieve the goal of fully understanding the risk and putting in place appropriate mitigation measures. And if we choose to follow this path, how do we ensure that risks implicit in the development of such countermeasures are themselves controlled?

Natural catastrophes

First let us consider the term 'natural catastrophe'. This is usually taken to mean a game-changer: a sudden, often unpredictable event outside human control that totally changes the circumstances or environment in which we live. Natural catastrophes are usually accompanied by significant loss of life, although the loss can often be mitigated if appropriate warning and/or countermeasures are put in place. Of course, the phrase 'appropriate warning' implies a deeper knowledge of the phenomenon or of the factors that led to the critical event occurring.

Most of these events are short-lived, that is, they occur on time-scales of minutes, hours or at most days, and are (at least currently) beyond human control and any purely technical fix. An obvious solution is not to live in places where such events may occur – or, alternatively, to learn to live with the risk (whatever that means) and make the most of the benefits that may accrue, such as the availability of fertile land near volcanoes or flood plains, spectacular scenery, and so on. The acceptance of risk, and the almost fatalistic acceptance by some people to 'take the hit' if and when it occurs, perhaps on the assumption that the 'Big One' (earthquake, flood, volcanic eruption, etc.) won't occur in their lifetimes, is a common theme in our all too human response to rare, high-consequence events over which we, as individuals, have little or no direct experience or control.

FIGURE 7.1 North Sea flood of 31 January 1953. The image shows the
devastation wrought by the flood at Oude-Tonge, on the island of
Goeree-Overflakkee in the South Netherlands. (Image from Wikipedia
Commons.)

A further point is that, taking the world as a whole, ordinary or mundane natural disasters occur with sufficient frequency to permit a level of familiarity with the phenomena and the use of statistics to assess their impacts. Many natural catastrophes are very localised, for example confined to certain coastlines (Figure 7.1) or areas of known geological activity; and, unless one happens to live in such a region, can often be regarded with equanimity. Although we are familiar with many kinds of natural catastrophe, most of us – certainly those who live in the UK – can afford a sense of detachment, noting that when disasters occur they are likely only to affect those unlucky enough to be caught in the action.

In summary, natural catastrophes are sudden, uncontrollable, high-impact events, often occurring with little or no warning. They are mostly

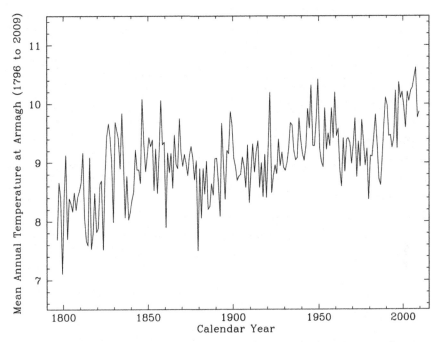

FIGURE 7.2 Climate change: an example of a slow-acting 'unnatural' natural catastrophe. Illustrated by the record of mean annual temperatures recorded at Armagh Observatory from 1796 to 2009. (Image credit: Armagh Observatory.)

local in scale, and very short-lived in duration compared with the average time intervals between them. Their global frequency means that they are amenable to scientific analysis and direct observation, and in this way we have opportunities to study the risks, receive warnings and anticipate their occurrence sufficiently far in advance to remove populations away from them if required.

There is of course another class of natural catastrophe, which I label 'unnatural' natural catastrophes. Here the signature of immediacy is often missing; rather, the catastrophe – for it is no less a disaster for those caught up in it – is the result of a slow-acting process, and the ultimate cause may be mankind's interaction with the environment. The most obvious contemporary example is climate change (Figure 7.2), a phenomenon that affects the whole globe (and may also have a significant extraterrestrial vector). In this case the risk affects every creature and organism on Earth, but because we have had no recent experience of such an event the risk is particularly difficult to quantify.

Unnatural natural catastrophes also elicit reactions such as denial ('maybe it will not happen') or fatalism ('there is nothing we can do about it'). Again, we must rely on science to understand the risk, but there is always much greater scientific uncertainty – partly because we have no recent experience to calibrate our theories, and partly also because we are forced by circumstance to extrapolate from rather limited knowledge and understanding. Here, perhaps, history can be a useful guide. Archaeology and written records can provide us with indirect evidence of events that took place thousands of years ago. Deciphering the clues and aligning them with projections from current theories may help significantly to advance scientific knowledge so far as rare natural catastrophes are concerned.

Risk

Next, consider the first element of the title of this article, namely 'Risk'. It is a word that has many different meanings in common parlance, a fact that has had the rather unfortunate result that when people use the word 'risk' we, and they, don't necessarily know what they are talking about! One has only to look at two dictionary definitions of the word to see the confusion that exists. For example, whereas *Chambers Twentieth Century Dictionary* gets it more or less right, as 'hazard, danger, chance of loss or injury; degree of probability of loss ...', the *Compact Oxford English Dictionary* merely states that risk is 'the possibility that something unpleasant will happen ...'. The UK Treasury, which also takes a keen interest in risk, defines it thus: 'Uncertainty in outcome, whether positive opportunity or negative threat, of actions and events ...'.

Whatever the precise definition, the key is to recognise and clearly separate the two elements that together make up our concept of 'risk', namely the event component and the frequency of the event. The closest, and in my view perhaps the best, analogy is to adopt an insurance perspective. Here, the precise nature of the event for which we seek insurance is specified in the small print of the insurance policy; and the insurance company

SCORE / FREQUENCY	IMPACT	1 Low	2 Low–Medium	3 Medium	4 Medium–High	5 High
5	High	5	10	15	20	25
4	Medium–High	4	8	12	16	20
3	Medium	3	6	9	12	15
2	Low–Medium	2	4	6	8	10
1	Low	1	2	3	4	5

FIGURE 7.3 Armagh Observatory risk matrix. The darkest colour represents a red 'high' risk; white represents a yellow 'medium' risk; and grey represents a 'green' low risk. (Image credit: Armagh Observatory.)

would know or be able to estimate from its claims history how frequently such events occur and what their cost was likely to be. Thus, we obtain an actuarial cost for the identified risk, which, with a bit of profit for the company, leads to the annual premium that you or I would pay.

This provides a relatively dispassionate way to assess risk, one that in the ideal case allows some events to be dismissed as lying below a *de minimis* threshold and others to be given correspondingly closer scrutiny. A monetary proxy for risk allows different kinds of risk to be ranked and a decision taken whether they are significant enough for us to be concerned about them. In other words, it enables us to see the wood for the trees.

Risk assessments are notoriously subjective; and, partly no doubt to provide the illusion of mathematical precision, estimates are usually presented in the form of a 'risk matrix', with rows (or sometimes columns) representing the perceived frequency of a given event, and columns (or sometimes rows) representing the perceived impact of that event occurring. Businesses and governments approve of this approach, which is illustrated in Figure 7.3 by the risk matrix that the Armagh Observatory is obliged by government to use.

The rubric associated with Figure 7.3 indicates that the highest 'impact', with a numerical value of five, might be caused by failure of key Observatory or Departmental objectives, or lead to financial loss exceeding several million pounds, or to significant public embarrassment to the Department and/or national media coverage (though sometimes we seek that), or attention from the Assembly or Public Accounts

Committee . . . or even death. On the frequency axis, low–medium (that is, a numerical value of two) means that the event might conceivably occur at some time, which actually means that it will probably occur once or twice; and in that sense the product of the two risk factors, in this case 5 x 2 = 10, leads to a 'red' or 'high' risk. Such a risk should always be mitigated, if possible.

In the context of natural catastrophes, which by their nature will almost certainly lead to 'death' and must 'conceivably occur at some time', these definitions are bound to place natural catastrophes in the red-risk, 'high' category, indicating that resources should always be provided to reduce the risk to an acceptable level. However, while governments encourage us to plan for the worst in the cases of pandemic influenza, storm or flood, much less frequent, but potentially very much larger natural catastrophes don't figure on our risk register. By some sleight of hand, they are deemed not 'our' responsibility, again raising the question – which of us is to look after such risks?

The risks that affect many people simultaneously are called 'societal risks', and because of the large range both in the frequency of occurrence of different events and of their respective impacts are usually presented in graphical form. Developing one of the points made earlier, namely that natural catastrophes are mostly fairly localised and occur rather suddenly and without warning, it is fortunate that we live in a world where the greater the number of people affected, the longer the recurrence time between events.

Figure 7.4 provides a graphical representation of risk, in which the relative impact and the relative likelihood of different kinds of event combine to indicate that electronic attacks, terrorist attacks on crowded places, and pandemic flu are all quite likely – that is, will occur within a human lifetime – whereas major industrial accidents are far less likely but may have a similarly high impact. In this way, we begin to see how risks can be ranked according to the objectively assessed criteria of frequency and impact.

Figure 7.5, taken from the Health and Safety Executive's 'Tolerability of Risk from Nuclear Power Stations' report (1992), presents what has now become a very common way to assess the impact of very rare, high-consequence events. This provides another way of looking at risk from

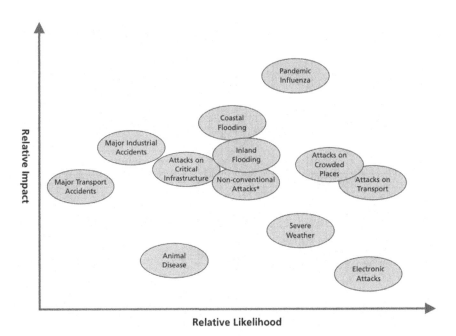

Relative Impact

Relative Likelihood

FIGURE 7.4 Location on the frequency–impact plane of various
high-consequence risks facing the United Kingdom. This is not the full range
of possible risks to the UK, but the location of each broad category of threat
nevertheless indicates the perceived risk that must be managed. For full
details see www.cabinetoffice.gov.uk/resource-library/national-risk-register.
(Image credit: Cabinet Office National Risk Register, © Crown copyright
2008.)

an insurance perspective, but with the unit of currency a human life. If,
for example, everyone could agree on the average value of a life (too
often this is narrowly interpreted as the 'economic value' of a life), then
together with the frequency of a given risk – or, to put it another way,
the frequency of events that might lead to a large number of fatalities –
we could determine how much money we should be prepared to pay to
avoid, if possible, such an event. For example, if a particular incident
were to lead to 100 deaths every 1,000 years, on average, and if this were
regarded as the limit of intolerability (that is, you could barely live with
this outcome), then if the value of a human life were £1.5 million, you
should be prepared to install countermeasures costing upwards of around
£150,000 a year in order to avoid that particular risk.

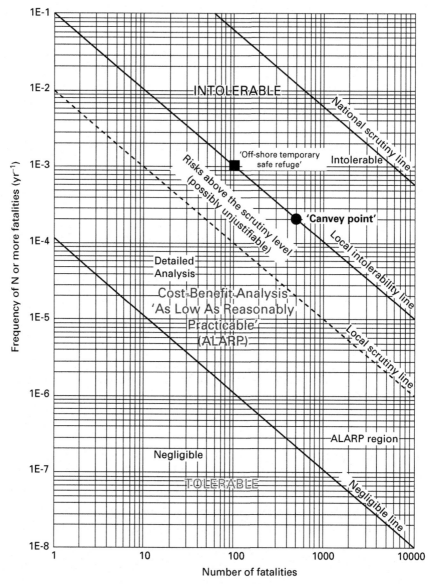

FIGURE 7.5 F–N criteria for societal risk. (Image credit: Figure adapted from Figure D1 of HSE, 1992. After Nigel Holloway, 1997 Spaceguard Meeting, Royal Greenwich Observatory, Cambridge.)

This approach has advantages, but raises many questions – not least what the value of a human life is, and what one's (or society's) risk appetite is. For example, if the events in question are very rare indeed, many decision-makers will take a pragmatic approach and 'gamble' that the risk will not crystallise on their watch, though such an approach, if continued, will likely end in disaster. Similarly, an individual's assessment of the value of their own life or that of a family member is likely to be much greater than £1.5 million! There are many ethical issues – for example to what extent can the value of a human life be measured in purely monetary terms and be assumed a universal constant? Does it depend on the lives in question; their income or employment; the good (or bad) that they do; their place of birth, nationality, and so on? And how do you apply the actuarial approach to situations of high risk involving large numbers of possibly simultaneous fatalities?

Leaving these complications aside, the idea of a Frequency–Number or 'F–N' diagram, showing the number of expected deaths versus the frequency of occurrence of a given event, provides a useful way of ranking different kinds of natural catastrophe. Risks can be deemed intolerable if the frequency of events leading to at least N deaths is too high, and tolerable, in other words below the negligible line, if the average number of lives at stake per year is close to zero. Between the lines of tolerable and intolerable you seek to reduce the risk to an acceptable level 'as low as reasonably practicable' (ALARP). And that's what we do in our daily lives so far as risk is concerned, as also do governments in respect of their regulatory regimes on behalf of society. Clearly, there are large uncertainties, but, despite shortcomings, an actuarial approach has the merit of allowing qualitatively different types of risk to be assigned an objective cost that can be more easily ranked and discussed.

Astronomy

We now leave the thin ice of ethics and move on to the apparently more secure ground of astronomy. First, our violent Universe potentially trumps any purely Earth-based cataclysm that you or I might care to name. One way of illustrating this is by the death of the dinosaurs (Figure 7.6), which occurred around 65 million years ago. The impact of

FIGURE 7.6 Death of the dinosaurs. The painting by astronomer Don Davis shows pterosaurs at the instant of collision of a 10-km-diameter asteroid with the Earth 65 million years ago, a catastrophe that is widely believed to have led to the mass extinction of species around this time, identified with the Cretaceous-Tertiary ('K/T') geological boundary. (Image credit: Don Davis, NASA.)

a comet or an asteroid on the Earth wiped out large numbers of species, changing the course of evolution of life on Earth. In particular, it provided an opportunity for mammals and eventually humans to appear – so from a purely selfish point of view the impact was clearly a 'Good Thing'!

Nowadays everybody is aware that the Earth – like the Moon – is a bombarded planet. For every crater you see on the Moon, the Earth will have been struck approximately twenty times as often because of the relative size of the two objects. The frequency of large impact craters on Earth is illustrated in Figure 7.7. Some areas of the Earth's surface, such as parts of Africa, Australia and North America, are very, very old and still show evidence of impacts that have occurred over geologic time. There

Earth impact sites

Design by David Rajmon using Impact database v.2010.1
and NASA Blue Marble topographic map - 15 May 2010.

Status:

● Confirmed with shock or chemical evidence

● Highly probable based on geological evidence

○ Probable

Diameter (km):

· <10   ● 50–100

● 10–50   ● 100–300

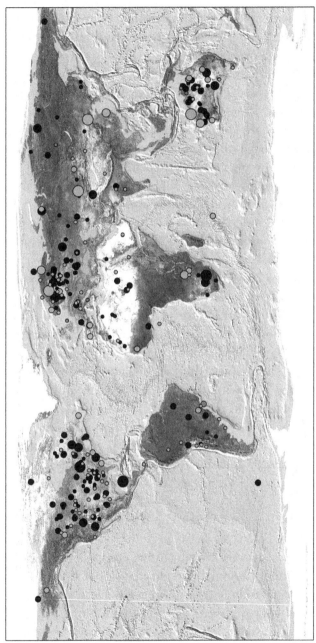

FIGURE 7.7 Bombarded Earth, showing sites of identified, highly probable and probable impact craters as at 16 May 2010. (Image credit: David Rajmon, Impact Database 2010.1. Online at http://impacts.rajmon.cz.)

are nearly 200 recognised large impact craters on the Earth, a figure consistent with the Earth being hit by a 'Big One', that is, a 'dinosaur-killer' capable of causing a global mass extinction of species, roughly once every 100 million years or so.

In the distant past, soon after the Earth was formed, the rate of large-body impacts was much higher, and as a consequence the newly formed Earth would have been sterilised by the heat liberated by frequent impacts. Today, 4.5 billion years after the formation of the Earth, occasional large-body impacts may still occur with the capacity to produce widespread devastation. How are we to assess such a natural catastrophe? In terms of actuarial risk, such an event would formally have an infinite cost (that is, it would be intolerable in every sense of the word), and so – even though it is a very rare event – the risk would be mathematically unbounded and we should do everything possible to avoid its occurrence.

The objects that produce these kinds of impacts are known to astronomers as Near-Earth Objects (NEOs), due to the fact that their orbits come close to or cross that of the Earth. They are shown in Figure 7.8. Briefly, NEOs are any astronomically 'small' body that can pass close to Earth. The size of these observed objects covers a very large range – from a few tens of metres up to tens of kilometres or more.

NEOs constitute a very diverse population, including both comets and asteroids, and fragments thereof; 'dead' or devolatilised (or temporarily inactive) comets; and occasional, but very rare, 'giant' comets (that is, comets with diameters larger than about 100 km). At the lower end of the size range the population of NEOs merges into that of meteoroids and interplanetary dust, the total mass influx of these small particles on Earth being about 1 kg per second, or some tens of thousands of tonnes of material per year.

Where do they come from? The asteroids by and large come from the main asteroid belt, lying between Mars and Jupiter in the solar system. The dynamical process by which this occurs is rather complicated and has only recently begun to be elucidated, but it usually begins with a catastrophic collision between two asteroids in the main belt. This is a random and unpredictable event and the resulting fragments move into new, possibly unstable orbits, some of which may become planet-crossing, eventually Earth-crossing and possibly Earth-colliding. It is evident that

FIGURE 7.8 Left: Composite image of the nucleus of Halley's comet taken during the Comet Halley encounter of 13–14 March 1986. Halley's comet is approximately 15 km long and 8 km wide. (Image credit: H. U. Keller, Halley Multicolour Camera, MPAe; ESA/Giotto.)
Right: Mosaic of the northern hemisphere of the near-Earth asteroid Eros, taken by the NASA Near-Earth Asteroid Rendezvous (NEAR-Shoemaker) spacecraft on 29 February 2000. Eros is approximately 34 km long and 11 km wide. (Image credit: Johns Hopkins University, Applied Physics Laboratory, NASA/NEAR-Shoemaker.)

this process, which has the potential to change the course of evolution of life on Earth, introduces a high degree of contingency in how life on any such bombarded planet might evolve.

The comets have a variety of sources. The main one is the Oort cloud, a vast swarm of dust-and-ice comet nuclei extending halfway to the nearest star, and yet still part of the solar system. An important secondary source is the Edgeworth-Kuiper belt, a thousand times closer in the region immediately beyond Neptune. Comets, too, are subject to the vagaries of occasional collisions, as well as to the effects of loss of volatile material from the central nucleus. Their orbits are more uncertain in the long term owing to perturbations by occasional 'random' close approaches of distant stars and molecular clouds to our solar system, and by the systematic gravitational perturbations of the Galaxy as a whole.

If one asks how many of these objects there are and why the comet and asteroid impact hazard has recently come to prominence, the answer is that our knowledge has increased dramatically within the last twenty years or so. In this time there has been a very rapid increase in the number of known (that is, discovered) Earth-crossing asteroids: from approximately 135 in 1990 to around 7,000 at the time of writing. Among these NEOs the number with average diameters larger than about a kilometre is thought to be of the order of 1,000. There is of course some uncertainty about that number, but it is now widely accepted that it is known to be rather better than a factor of two. This, together with knowledge of the NEO orbits, enables astronomers to estimate the average frequency of collision of such bodies with the Earth; the result is that one such impact occurs roughly every 200,000 years on average. In addition to these kilometre-sized objects, there is a further more poorly understood population of comets and extinct comet nuclei, and a very large number of smaller bodies, the total number increasing roughly as the inverse square of the diameter down to 50 or 100 metres or so.

What effects would one of these objects produce were it to impact the Earth? The size of the astronomically smallest objects of any real significance so far as impacts are concerned is in the range 30–100 metres, and the size of the largest observed NEOs extends up to that of a terrestrial mountain (that is, up to several tens of kilometres). At the lower end of this size range the kinetic energies of impact are of the order of 10–100 megatons, and if they reached the ground (which not all of them will) the objects would make craters with sizes up to a kilometre across. A 'rule of thumb' is that the size of the crater is approximately ten to twenty times the size of the object. Other things (e.g. mass) being equal, comets are more dangerous than asteroids because on average they have much higher impact velocities than asteroids. On the other hand, comets are widely believed to be less dense than asteroids, and so, size for size, the effects of the two classes of object are thought to be similar.

For object diameters much larger than 30–100 metres most, if on target, will reach the ground, producing craters bigger than a few kilometres across. Sub-kilometre-size objects would destroy areas the size of a large city or a small state or province. Oceanic impacts would produce tsunamis, and as one moves up in size the kinetic energies of impact become almost unimaginable. The size of craters resulting from the impact of kilometre-sized bodies and larger range upwards from around 20 kilometres, and the implied giant tsunamis would have a reach extending to ocean scales.

The frequency of comet or asteroid impacts with diameters greater than a critical value of the order of 0.5 to 2 kilometres is a key parameter in the evaluation of the risk. For sizes larger than this, the impacts will have global consequences wherever they hit. Smaller objects cause local devastation, but – just as with 'ordinary' natural catastrophes – the parts of the world not immediately affected will probably not be affected at all. The largest known NEOs, with sizes up to 10 or more kilometres would produce environmental effects of such a magnitude that they could produce a mass extinction of life on Earth.

It is fortunate that the largest objects are relatively few in number and the most infrequent among impactors; it is fortunate too that they are also the easiest objects to discover in space. This suggests that the evolution of life on Earth has benefited from a favourable conjunction of events, in particular the time since humans have evolved is only a few million years – which is short compared with the average time-interval between really large impacts. During this time (in fact within the last hundred years) we have developed the knowledge and technical capacity to discover essentially all the most dangerous objects in near-Earth space.

We humans are therefore living at a very special time in Earth history: for the first time in the history of life on Earth, a species has developed that has the scientific and technical knowledge broadly to understand its place in space and the wider Universe; and at the same time has the technological capacity in principle to do something about the risk of rare, massive impacts. However, the issue is not of particularly urgent concern: we do not know of any large comet or asteroid that is currently on an orbit destined to collide with the Earth within the next hundred years or so. Moreover, if the mean interval between really big impacts is tens or perhaps hundreds of millions of years we would have to be very unlucky indeed to be living at such a time of crisis.

Of course, our understanding of the environmental effects of more frequent but still massive impacts is still at a very rudimentary stage, and we have – fortunately – not been able to test our theories in this regime. Impacts of kilometre-size bodies on planets do occur, however, and a few

FIGURE 7.9 Impact of Comet Shoemaker-Levy 9 on Jupiter. Comet D/1993 F2 (Shoemaker-Levy 9) broke into more than twenty fragments which collided with Jupiter during the period 16–22 July 1994. The impacts produced long-lived atmospheric 'scars' visible from Earth. This image of Jupiter with the Hubble Space Telescope Planetary Camera shows five large impact sites and three small ones, ranging in size from several hundred kilometres up to Earth-size. (Image credit: NASA/ESA Hubble Space Telescope.)

years ago we had the opportunity to witness a sequence of such impacts on Jupiter, namely the impact of fragments of the tidally disrupted Comet Shoemaker-Levy 9 in July 1994. Figure 7.9 illustrates the Earth-scale atmospheric effects produced by these events, and it is partly as a result of this experience that some commentators now consider the 'critical' size of an impactor necessary to produce a devastating global effect on Earth so far as the survival of civilisation is concerned (for example through a rapid impact-induced climate change) as lying closer to 0.5 km than 2.0 km.

Another well-known example is the case of the twentieth-century Tunguska event, which in June 1908 flattened and destroyed a forested area in Siberia roughly equal to the area of Greater London. It had a blast equivalent of approximately 3–10 megatons and, had it landed over London, it would clearly have destroyed that whole area and much of the surrounding districts. Leaving aside the potential loss of life, the economic consequences of such an impact, negligible in global terms, would influence the affected nation's prosperity for years.

FIGURE 7.10 Left: Fall of the Sikhote-Alin meteorite on 12 February 1947, from the painting in the Russian Academy of Sciences. (Image courtesy Yu. A. Shukolyukov.)
Right: Totem pole erected close to the Tunguska 'ground zero'. According to mythology, Agby is the Siberian 'god' who brings fire to the forest.

The left panel of Figure 7.10 shows another instance, this time the impact of a rather smaller object, in the large-meteorite class, which encountered Earth in 1947. It is a painting from the Russian Academy of Sciences showing the Sikhote-Alin meteorite. At right is the totem pole erected tongue-in-cheek by Russian scientists close to the Tunguska 'ground zero'. The totem pole represents the Siberian fire god 'Agby' – he who brings fire to the forest – and there is already a thriving modern mythology that if one does not leave a trinket or personal possession at Agby's feet, one will never return to this 'sacred' site. It is amusing to note that many Western scientists travel thousands of kilometres, as if in pilgrimage, to the area in order to inspect the site and search for traces of the impactor.

Cost of impacts

With these examples in mind, let us now estimate the actuarial risk posed by NEOs. To do this, we assume there to be roughly 1,500 objects larger than 1 km in diameter, each capable of causing a global catastrophe, for example rapid climate change and a subsequent devastating effect on global civilisation. The mean impact probability is of the order of one in several hundred million per year per object. Thus, the average rate of impacts is roughly one event every 200,000 years (for objects larger than 1 km in diameter); and if a quarter of the UK's population of 60 million is assumed to die as a result of such an impact, and each life is valued at £1.5 million, the actuarial risk – or cost – of NEO impacts to the UK alone becomes approximately £100 million per year. Note that a proportionate cost is incurred by other nations, and the cost is incurred wherever the impactor happens to land: the effects of impacts by objects larger than a kilometre in diameter are global.

This raises a number of questions so far as risk and natural catastrophes are concerned. Clearly the annual cost (less than the cost of a large passenger jet) is affordable, and there are also many things we can begin to do to address the problem (such as discover the potentially hazardous asteroids in advance of any impact, predict where and when the next impact will occur and/or relocate people who happen to live close to 'ground zero', and so on). There is even the possibility of deflecting the asteroid in space so that it misses the Earth entirely, although this raises the question of who controls such asteroid deflection technology and whether the same technology could perhaps be used for clandestine offensive, rather than defensive, purposes.

Another point is that the cost of this type of natural catastrophe is, in fact, much higher than has already been calculated, that is, the risk is actually greater than estimated. This is because the largest impacts may lead to extinction of the human race, and in this sense the risk is unbounded. Placing the calculated NEO risk on the F–N diagram shown in Figure 7.5 indicates that asteroids easily fall in the 'Intolerable' part of the figure. Moreover, because the risk is larger than that, reason tells us we should develop an action plan to reduce or eliminate it. By the same token, reason also tells us that that the initial cost of developing such a plan could range up to several hundred million pounds per year, for the UK alone, and still provide good value for money.

Let me emphasise that this is not an argument to fund astronomy (!), but it demonstrates the value of funding 'pure' research, not really knowing what future benefits it will bring. In this case, astronomers serendipitously discovered a significant NEO impact hazard to civilisation having an actuarial cost to the UK alone of the order of £100 million per year. What we do with the information is another question, and one that, like most extreme cases, goes to the heart of the problem. An issue that might be considered, for example, is the question of our risk appetite or (some might say) our risk indigestion. Note that the chance of a kilometre-size impact on Earth within our lifetimes is extremely remote, far less than the probability of risks that we routinely accept as individuals on a daily basis (for example, a person in their mid-fifties has a *daily* risk of dying of around one in 200,000). A pragmatic response – perhaps the reaction of most people – would be to ignore the lowest probability high-consequence risks as lying below one's individual level of concern.

If this turns out to be humanity's considered reaction to the problem, perhaps the lesson is that – as with many modern scientific discoveries – our 'instinct' is letting us down, or, to put it another way: our 'gut' has not kept pace with our brains. We are culturally attuned to ignoring low-probability hazards that might significantly affect us as individuals, families or small groups, often preferring simply to get on with our lives rather than making a possibly uncomfortable change to our lifestyle to avoid the risk. Examples such as smoking, crossing the road, driving while using a mobile phone, flying, and so on, immediately come to mind. With these ingrained habits there is a risk that we adopt the same response to low-probability high-consequence societal risks, even when the actuarial risk is high and when a particular incident could affect millions or perhaps billions of people at the same time.

To conclude this section, let me briefly emphasise a further important point about the NEO impact hazard, namely its singular nature. As well as producing a potentially unbounded risk, impacts are highly predictable, often years or decades in advance, provided we have sufficient knowledge of the NEO ensemble; in short, NEO impacts are avoidable given enough warning. One could, for example, remove the affected population from 'ground zero'; stockpile food supplies for the years when food would be scarce; or even engage in a 'star wars' deflection of the NEO in space, so that it never hits the Earth. Considering that the technology exists to rendezvous with comets and asteroids in space, and even to fire objects into them, it is clear that most of this risk – potentially the most serious risk we have yet faced as a species – could be mitigated.

Broader astronomical context

Rather than dwell on the effects of comet or asteroid impacts, or the possible effects on Earth of the accretion of interplanetary dust produced by the evolution of comets or by collisions of asteroids in the main belt, let me finally describe some of the continuing uncertainties underlying our present understanding of the astronomical context in which NEO impacts occur.

It is widely recognised that astronomy is currently experiencing a 'Golden Age', in which the separate strands of human endeavour that motivate interest in the subject, for example the 'cosmological or quasi-religious' strand, the 'astrophysics' strand and the 'practical or spin-off' strand, have come together to produce incredibly rapid progress and great leaps in understanding. Astronomy plays an important cultural role as an imagination driver, not just in science but also in the humanities, art and history, stimulating the work worldwide of artists, poets, musicians and philosophers.

In any subject that is advancing so fast, there are bound to be errors and uncertainties. In fact, it is part of an astronomer's job to dismiss old theories and replace them with new, hopefully better understanding, and there is no reason to think this has finished. Up to now I have described what might be called the 'standard' model of the NEO impact hazard; but if we are intent on assessing the hazard in the long term, which involves time-scales of hundreds or thousands of years, or more, we really must take a more strategic view. This reflects the point famously made by

Donald Rumsfeld about the 'known knowns', the 'known unknowns', and the unknowns that we do not even know exist. How do we fold such 'systematic' scientific uncertainties into a correct assessment of the long-term risk posed by natural catastrophes?

Let me illustrate the point by describing some recent advances in solar-system astronomy that may yet prove to be an important element in assessing the extraterrestrial impact hazard. Astronomers have discovered that giant comets exist as part of a very broad size distribution of planet-crossing objects extending to dimensions much greater than 100 kilometres in diameter. The orbits of these objects, their number in the inner solar system and their detailed physical characteristics all vary on time-scales of thousands of years, that is, on time-scales of human concern. Such objects also contribute to the fluctuating population of NEOs, which themselves are only a relatively recently discovered population of Earth-interacting bodies. And comets have the peculiar characteristic that their evolution and decay lead to the production of narrow trails of debris, and therefore to non-random impacts on Earth, evidenced by the familiar annual meteor showers, the Shoemaker-Levy 9 event on Jupiter, and the series of almost daily small-comet impacts on the Sun, originating from the hierarchical fragmentation of a large Sun-grazing progenitor thousands of years ago.

Cometary evolution is highly chaotic and therefore unpredictable in the long term. Moreover, as evidenced by the Shoemaker-Levy 9 event and examples where comets have split into two or more pieces, comets are very fragile, easily broken up in space and with short physical lifetimes of perhaps only a few thousand years in short-period Earth-crossing orbits. Thus, the comets we see are very different from those that our ancestors would have seen 4,000 or 5,000 years ago.

An example that illustrates this unpredictability is an object called Chiron, which is actually one of a class of newly discovered solar-system objects called Centaurs. Its present orbit has a perihelion distance (the closest point to the Sun) slightly inside the orbit of Saturn, and an orbital period of around fifty years. If one models the evolution of a large number of bodies with very similar orbits to the real Chiron, the result illustrates the enormous uncertainty in predicting the evolution of an individual object over very long time-scales. The orbits are chaotic, which means that very small changes in the initial conditions of the orbit or in the circumstances of the comet's orbital evolution, quickly lead to gross differences in the objects' predicted future and past orbital evolution. In the case of a Centaur such as Chiron, there is a chance that it may have been a short-period Earth-crossing comet for some thousands of years as recently as 75,000 years ago.

What would such an object have looked like? A Centaur such as Chiron is a very massive object, with a diameter of the order of 200 kilometres, and the amount of dust that such an object could deposit in the inner solar system during a period of evolution as a short-period comet is huge. It is possible that it might shed fragments of ordinary comet size (i.e. kilometres across) as well as dust, and that these might have contributed to a heightened space density of solid objects in the inner solar system and to a temporary enhancement in the rate of accretion of such bodies – and hence the impact hazard – on Earth.

Such a scenario is simply not accounted for in the present 'standard' picture of the risks posed by the current NEO population, but this is precisely the sort of bigger picture that must be developed if we are to obtain a full understanding of our place, and that of the Earth, in the cosmos.

It is here that arguments from history and perhaps archaeology too may help to inform astronomers and increase our understanding of the types of phenomena that humans may have witnessed, but of which we now have essentially no knowledge. There are many puzzling 'mysteries' concerning the earliest Greek descriptions of the cosmos, for example Anaximander's view of 'stars'; Aristotle's description of the Milky Way as lying in the sublunary zone and being an accumulation product of the disintegration of many comets; and other authors' identification of the Milky Way as the former path of the Sun. None of these views can readily be reconciled with our understanding of the solar system unless the 'sky' in those days was somehow different, perhaps more active in terms of cometary and meteoric phenomena than it is now, leading to a possible 'confusion' between what was once a much brighter zodiacal light and the present Milky Way. In this case, modern astronomy would have a lot to teach historians as well.

Conclusions

Studies of natural catastrophes caused by extraterrestrial impacts show that these phenomena constitute a unique risk. The extraterrestrial impact hazard provides a conjunction of difficulties for conventional risk analysis. We do not have any recent experience of such impacts, except perhaps through historical records, and their potentially unbounded consequences and global reach would be intolerable except that they represent very low-probability events. The existence of such a threat raises questions such as which of the nations has the responsibility to mitigate the threat, and who controls the resulting knowledge and technology.

The actuarial approach provides a rational way to rank risks of very diverse types and character, and in principle can be applied to all risks so long as one can agree the costs. As with any market, the perceived costs will vary with fashion and time (perhaps that is a strength rather than a weakness), facilitating a focus on risks that are objectively assessed as most important. Our present understanding of the majority of high-consequence, low-probability risks remains very uncertain, and options to mitigate the majority of natural catastrophes are very limited.

The foreseeable extraterrestrial impact hazard, however, is unique in that in most cases it should be possible to predict with precision the time and location of the large-body impact, and it is likely that the largest such impactors would be discoverable decades, if not centuries in advance of any impact. The biggest impactors have implications for the survival of civilisation and the human race, and perhaps also for the future evolution of life on Earth. If humanity were to develop technology to mitigate this threat, then we – uniquely among all life forms that have ever existed on the planet – would have largely inoculated ourselves against a major external driver of evolutionary change.

The analysis also shows that as a result of undertaking curiosity-driven research we live at a 'special time' in the history of life on Earth: we recognise Earth's place in the Universe; we recognise that Earth is a bombarded planet; and that Earth is an 'open' system in touch with its near-space environment. This understanding represents a significant paradigm shift, though one that is difficult to see because we are living through it. We also recognise that controlling impacts holds the key to the long-term survival of civilisation, even to the long-term survival of life on Earth; and a species – namely us – has the knowledge to compute and assess the risk.

So, for the first time in the 3.8-billion-year history of life on Earth these facts are broadly known. The historian Stephen Toulmin in his book *The Return to Cosmology* captured this sense of our position when he wrote (p. 260):

> Human beings, like all other living creatures on earth, are the beneficiaries of history ... our fate within this historical scheme depends ... on the adaptiveness of our behaviour ... [and] on the use that we make of our intelligence in dealing with our place in Nature.

It will be interesting to see whether we rise to the challenge of 'the long-view' and take the steps necessary to mitigate the potentially unbounded risks to life on Earth posed by extraterrestrial impacts.

Acknowledgements

I thank the organisers of the Darwin Lecture series for the invitation to provide this lecture and for their help in producing this manuscript. Astronomy at Armagh Observatory is funded by the Northern Ireland Department of Culture, Arts and Leisure.

References/Further reading

ARTICLES AND REPORTS CONCERNING RISK IN GENERAL

Government Policy on the Management of Risk (2006) House of Lords Select Committee on Economic Affairs, 5th Report of Session 2005–06, HL Paper 183-I. Available online at: www.publications.parliament.uk/pa/ld200506/ldselect/ldeconaf/183/183i.pdf.

National Risk Register of Civil Emergencies (2010) Cabinet Office. Available online at: www.cabinetoffice.gov.uk/resource–library/national-risk-register.

Safety in Numbers? (1996) Parliamentary Office of Science and Technology Report No. 81. Available online at: www.parliament.uk/documents/post/pn081.pdf.

The Tolerability of Risk from Nuclear Power Stations. (1992), Health and
Safety Executive (HSE). Available online at: www.hse.gov.uk/
nuclear/tolerability.pdf.

ARTICLES AND REPORTS CONCERNING RISK AND NEOS

Bailey, M. E., Clube, S. V. M., Hahn, G., Napier, W. M. and Valsecchi,
G. B. (1994) 'Hazards due to comets: climate and short-term
catastrophism', in T. Gehrels (ed.), *Hazards Due to Comets and
Asteroids,* Tucson and London: University of Arizona Press,
pp. 479–533.
Canavan, G. H. (1994) 'Cost and benefit of near-earth object detection
and interception', in Gehrels (ed.), *Hazards,* pp. 1157–89.
Chapman, C. R. (2004) 'The hazard of near-earth asteroid impacts on
Earth', *Earth and Planetary Science Letters,* 222: 1–15.
Chapman, C. R. and Morrison, D. (1994) 'Impacts on the Earth by
asteroids and comets: assessing the hazard', *Nature* 367:
33–40.
Gehrels, T. (ed.) (1994) *Hazards Due to Comets and Asteroids.* Tucson and
London: University of Arizona Press.
Near Earth Objects – NEOs (1999) Parliamentary Office of Science and
Technology Report No. 126. Available online at: www.parliament.
uk/documents/post/pn126.pdf.
Remo, J. L. (1997) 'Near-Earth objects: The United Nations international
conference', *Annals of the New York Academy of Sciences* 822.

BOOKS AND ARTICLES DESCRIBING NATURAL
CATASTROPHES IN A BROADER HISTORICAL CONTEXT

Bailey, M. E. (1995) 'Recent results in cometary astronomy: implications
for the ancient sky', *Vistas in Astronomy* 39: 647–71.
Bailey, M. E., Clube, S. V. M. and Napier, W. M. (1990) *The Origin of
Comets.* Oxford: Pergamon Press.
Greene, M. T. (1992) *Natural Knowledge in Preclassical Antiquity.*
Baltimore and London: Johns Hopkins University Press.
Huggett, R. (1989) *Cataclysms and Earth History: The Development of
Diluvialism.* Oxford: Clarendon Press.
Nur, A. (2008) *Apocalypse: Earthquakes, Archaeology, and the Wrath of God.*
Princeton University Press.
Peiser, B. J., Palmer, T. and Bailey, M. E. (1998) *Natural Catastrophes
During Bronze Age Civilizations: Archaeological, Geological,*

Mark Bailey

Astronomical and Cultural Perspectives. British Archaeological
Reports, No. S728. Oxford: Archaeopress.
Toulmin, S. (1985) *The Return to Cosmology: Postmodern Science and the
Theology of Nature.* Berkeley, Los Angeles and London: University of
California Press.

8 Risk in the context of (human-induced) climate change

ROBERT WATSON

Overview

Most countries are attempting to achieve environmentally and socially sustainable economic growth, coupled with food, water and energy security at a time of enormous global changes, including environmental degradation at the local, regional and global scale. Key issues include climate change, loss of biodiversity and ecosystem services (provisioning, regulating, cultural and supporting), local and regional air pollution, and land and water degradation.

There is no doubt that the Earth's climate is changing and it is very likely that most of the observed changes in the last fifty years are due to human activities. Cost-effective and equitable approaches to address climate change exist or can be developed, but will require political will and moral leadership. A combination of technological and behavioural changes, coupled with pricing and effective policies (including regulatory policies), are needed to address this global challenge at all spatial scales, that is, local, national and international, and across sectors.

The risks associated with climate change

Climate change is an environment, development and security issue, potentially risking undermining:

- food, water and human security
- the economy (loss of natural capital)
- poverty alleviation and the livelihoods of the poor
- human health
- efforts to reduce the loss of biodiversity and ecosystem degradation
- personal, national and regional security.

159

Climate change is an inter- and intra-generational equity issue and risks adversely affecting developing countries and poor people in developing countries as well as future generations. Climate change cannot be considered in isolation from other global, regional and local environmental issues, namely loss of biodiversity and ecosystem degradation, deforestation and forest degradation, desertification, local and regional air and water quality, and stratospheric ozone depletion. These environmental issues are closely interlinked, and hence the policies to address them should be so too. It is essential to ensure that national and global climate change policies and technologies impact positively, and not negatively, on other aspects of the environment and human well-being.

Climate change: the current state of knowledge and risks of future changes

There is no doubt that the atmospheric concentrations of greenhouse gases (e.g., carbon dioxide, methane and nitrous oxide) have increased significantly over the past 150 years primarily due to human activities. These gases are radiatively active and absorb and trap outgoing infra-red radiation from the Earth's surface and hence, based on simple physics, the Earth's atmosphere must respond by warming. At the same time, the atmospheric concentration of sulphate aerosols, which tend to cool the planet by reflection of solar radiation as it passes through the atmosphere, has also increased due to emissions of sulphur dioxide, offsetting some of the warming due to the greenhouse gases. The only question is when, where and by how much the temperature will increase.

The International Panel on Climate Change (IPCC) Working Group I (2007) concluded that the global temperature data and analyses are robust, with increasingly variable and extreme temperatures. While a number of scientists argue that some of the land temperature data are contaminated and unreliable because of the urban heat island effect and movement of observational sites (the scientists who have reported these trends in the peer-review literature and IPCC argue that these effects are taken into account). Ocean data, and balloon and satellite data also show an increasingly warmer world (these data sets are clearly free from any potential contamination from an urban heat island effect). In addition, the evidence for a changing climate over the past 100 years also comes from observed changes in retreating mountain glaciers throughout most of the world, rising sea levels, a decline in the extent and thickness of Arctic sea ice in summer, melting of the Greenland ice sheet, changing precipitation patterns, increasing frequency of extreme weather events, such as heatwaves, floods and droughts; intensification of cyclonic events, such as hurricanes in the Atlantic; and changes in vegetation and the behaviour of wildlife.

The key question is the cause of the observed changes in temperature and other climatic parameters. The IPCC Working Group I (2007) concluded that it is very likely (>90 per cent certain) that most of the observed changes over the past fifty to sixty years are due to human activities, and that the observed changes cannot be explained by known natural phenomena, such as changes in solar radiation. That these changes will continue regionally and globally is now inevitable. Global mean surface temperature is projected to increase by 1.4°C to 6.4°C between 2000 and 2100. Temperatures in land areas in the high northern latitudes are expected to increase by 4–5°C by 2090 even under low-carbon emission scenarios, and by up to 10°C on average under high-carbon emission scenarios. Precipitation is more difficult to predict – however in general it is likely to increase at high latitudes and in the tropics and decrease significantly throughout much of the sub-tropics.

Climate change: the risks of adverse impacts

Future increases in greenhouse gas concentrations are projected to be accompanied by increased climate variability and more extreme climatic events, leading in general to adverse impacts on agriculture, water quantity and quality, coastal erosion, loss of biodiversity and degradation of ecosystem services. The impacts of climate change are likely to be extensive, primarily negative and to cut across many sectors, with the impacts being most severe in developing countries, and most likely to affect the poorest people. Hence, climate change is not only an environmental issue, but a development and security issue. The impacts of human-induced climate change could include:

- A longer thermal growing season at temperate latitudes likely leading to increased agricultural productivity for temperature changes below 2–3°C, but decreased productivity with larger changes. However, agricultural productivity will probably be negatively impacted by almost any warming throughout the tropics and sub-tropics, which are currently areas of high hunger and malnutrition. Increasing ocean temperatures, coupled with ocean acidification are likely to have adverse impacts on fisheries and on food security.
- Decreased water availability and water quality in many arid and semi-arid regions, as well as increased risk of floods and droughts in many regions, with adverse effects on water security.
- Loss of biodiversity, and adverse affects on most ecological systems, especially coral reefs and high-latitude and high-altitude ecosystems, resulting in potentially significant degradation of ecosystem goods and services and loss of key ecosystem services essential to human well-being and the economy.
- Adverse effects on human health through the increased incidence of vector- (e.g., malaria and dengue) and water-borne (e.g., cholera) diseases, heat stress mortality, threats to nutrition in developing countries, and increases in extreme weather event deaths.
- Adverse effects on human settlements due to flooding, coastal erosion and sea-level rise, with tens of millions of people being displaced.

Climate change: risks to food security and agricultural production

Recent trends in food production and prices are illustrated in Figure 8.1. Total food production has nearly trebled since 1960, per capita production has increased by about 30 per cent and food prices and the percentage of undernourished people have fallen, but the benefits have been uneven, and by 2003 about 815 million people still went to bed hungry each night. Furthermore, intensive and extensive food production has caused significant environmental degradation, including a significant contributor to greenhouse gas emissions and loss of biodiversity and degradation of ecosystem services (IAASTD, 2009).

Food prices increased during the last two years (2008–2010) for a number of reasons that are unlikely to disappear in the coming decades:

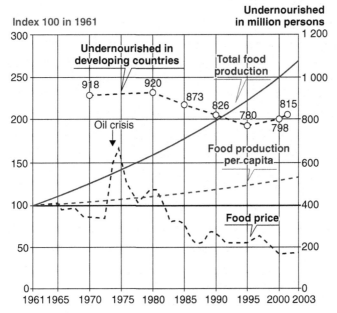

FIGURE 8.1 Global production, prices and undernourishment (taken from Millennium Ecosystem Assessment, 2005). Food production more than doubled (an increase of over 160 per cent) from 1961 to 2003. Over this period, food prices fell by half, while the number of undernourished persons declined only 12 per cent.

- poor harvests due to variable weather that are possibly related to human-induced climate change;
- high energy prices, increasing the cost of mechanisation and fertilisers;
- low value of the dollar;
- low stocks and possible speculation on the commodity markets;
- export bans from some large exporting countries to protect domestic supplies;
- increased production of biofuels, such as bio-ethanol from maize in the USA;
- increased demand in rapidly growing economies.

These increased prices pushed another 100 million people into hunger, and the recent economic downturn has added another 100 million under-nourished people.

The demand for food will likely double in the next twenty-five to fifty years, primarily in developing countries. Furthermore, the type and nutritional quality of food demanded will change, for example, demand for meat increasing. We need sustained growth in the agricultural sector to feed the world, enhance rural livelihoods and stimulate economic growth. Yet these new demands are arising at a time when, in addition to the challenges highlighted above, the world may have less agricultural labour due to disease and rural–urban migration, less water due to competition from other sectors, distorted trade policies due to OECD subsidies, land policy conflicts, loss of genetic, species, and ecosystem biodiversity, and increasing levels of air and water pollution.

Agriculture affects the environment: for example, tillage and irrigation methods can lead to erosion and salinisation of soils; rice and livestock production and use of inorganic fertilisers contribute to greenhouse gas emissions, and extensification of agricultural lands into grasslands and forests leads to loss of biodiversity at the genetic, species and landscape level, as well as an increase in greenhouse gas emissions. Environmental degradation in turn reduces agricultural productivity.

We can no longer think of agriculture in terms of production alone. We must acknowledge the multi-functionality of agriculture, and must place agriculture within a broad economic, social and environmental frame-work. We can feed the world with affordable food while providing a viable income for the farmer, but business-as-usual will not work. Most of today's hunger problems can be addressed with the appropriate use of current technologies, particularly agro-ecological practices (such as no/low till, integrated pest management and integrated natural resource management). These must be coupled with decreased post-harvest losses and global-scale policy reforms. This will include eliminating both OECD production subsidies and tariff escalation on processed products, and recognising the special needs of the least developed countries through non-reciprocal market access.

Emerging issues such as climate change and new plant and animal pests may increase our future need for higher productivity and may require advanced biotechnologies, including genetic modification, to address future food demands. However, the risks and benefits of these tools must be fully understood on a case-by-case basis. The public and private sectors should increase their investments in research and development, extension services and weather and market information.

Climate change – the risks of the loss of biodiversity (genetic, species and landscape level) and ecosystem services

Biodiversity is central to human well-being. Biodiversity provides a variety of ecosystem services that humankind relies on, including: provisioning (e.g. food, fresh water, wood and fibre, and fuel); regulating (e.g. of climate, flood, air quality, pollination and diseases); culture enhancing (e.g. aesthetic, spiritual, educational and recreational), and supporting (e.g. nutrient cycling, soil formation and primary production). These ecosystem services contribute to our well-being, including our security, health, social relations and freedom of choice and action.

Biodiversity loss at the genetic, species and landscape level is increasing for five reasons: habitat change (e.g. conversion of a forest or a grassland into agricultural land); climate change; invasive species, introduced either purposely or accidentally; over-exploitation (e.g. over-fishing); and pollution (e.g. phosphorus and nitrogen). The relative importance of these drivers of biodiversity and ecosystem change over the past 50–100 years is shown in Figure 8.2.

While climate change has not been a major cause of biodiversity loss or ecosystem degradation (except in the polar regions) over the last 100 years, it is likely to be a major threat in all biomes over the next 100 years.

Economic instruments, environmentally friendly technologies, national and international policies and behavioural change can help to reduce the loss of biodiversity and ecosystem services, and to reduce the impacts.

Firstly, we need to change the economic background to decision-making. To do so, we should account for the value of all ecosystem services, not just those bought and sold in the market; remove subsidies to agriculture, fisheries and energy that cause harm to people and the environment; and introduce payments to landowners for managing land in ways that protect ecosystem services that are of value to society, such as water quality and carbon storage. We should also establish market mechanisms that reduce nutrient releases and carbon emissions in cost-effective ways.

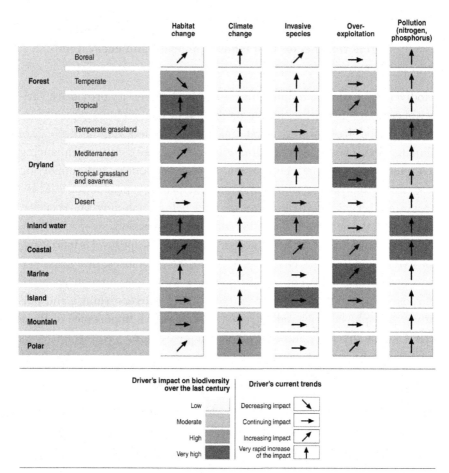

FIGURE 8.2 Main direct drivers of change in biodiversity and ecosystems (taken from Millenium Ecosystem Assessment, 2005). The cell shade indicates impact of each driver on biodiversity in each type of ecosystem over the past 50–100 years. High impact means that over the last century the particular driver has significantly altered biodiversity in that biome; low impact indicates that it has had little influence on biodiversity in the biome. The arrows indicate the trend in the driver. Horizontal arrows indicate a continuation of the current level of impact; diagonal and vertical arrows indicate progressively increasing or decreasing trends in impact.

Secondly, we should develop and use environmentally friendly technologies. We should invest in agricultural science and technology aimed at increasing food production with minimal harmful trade-offs and promote technologies that increase energy efficiency and reduce greenhouse gas emissions.

Thirdly, we should improve policy, planning and management. To do this, we must integrate decision-making between departments and sectors, as well as between international institutions and organisations, and include sound management of ecosystem services in all planning decisions. We should empower marginalised groups to influence decisions that affect ecosystem services, and recognise local communities' ownership of natural resources. We should establish additional protected areas and use all relevant forms of knowledge and information about ecosystems in decision-making, including the knowledge of local and indigenous groups.

Finally, we must influence individual behaviour. We can do this by providing public education on why and how to reduce consumption of threatened ecosystem services, establishing reliable certification systems to give people the choice to buy sustainably harvested products, and by providing access to information about ecosystems and decisions affecting their services.

Climate change: risks to water scarcity

Projections show that by 2025 over half of the world's population will live in places that are subject to severe water stress. This is irrespective of climate change, which will exacerbate the situation. Water quality is declining in many parts of the world. Approximately 50–60 per cent of wetlands have been lost. Human-induced climate change is projected to decrease water quality and availability in many arid and semi-arid regions and increase the threats posed by floods and droughts in most parts of the world. This will have far-reaching implications, including for agriculture, where 70 per cent of all fresh water is currently used for irrigation, and where 15–35 per cent of irrigation water use already exceeds supply and is thus unsustainable.

Fresh-water availability is spatially variable and scarce, particularly in many regions of Africa and Asia. Numerous dry regions, including many of the world's major 'food bowls', will likely become much drier even under medium levels of climate change. Glacier melt, which is a critically important source of water for many developing countries, will probably decrease and exacerbate this problem over the long term. Run-off will decrease in many places, especially in a number of the key food-producing areas of the world, due to decreased precipitation and increased evapo-transpiration. In contrast, precipitation is likely to increase in many of the world's wetter regions.

Cost recovery for water averages only 20 per cent, which poses a major problem because, when a scarce resource is not priced, it is often used inefficiently. The Dublin Principles, or a variant, should be implemented to help address the challenges associated with water scarcity. These include the:

- *Ecological principle:* river-basin management (often transnational); multi-sectoral management (agriculture, industry and households); and coupled land-and-water management.
- *Institutional principle:* comprehensive stakeholder involvement (state, private sector and civil society – especially women) in management action at the lowest level.
- *Instrument principle:* improved allocation and quality enhancement via incentives and economic principles.

Crucially, and most controversially (because in some societies it is thought to be immoral to charge for water), we must get water pricing right.

Climate change: risks to human security and equity

Climate change, coupled with other stresses, threatens human security in many parts of the world, potentially increasing the risk of conflict and in-country and out-of-country migration.

Climate change risks the spread of conflict by undermining the essentials of life for many poor people:

- Food shortages could increase where there is hunger and famine today.
- Water shortages could increase in areas where there are already water shortages.
- Natural resources could be depleted with loss of ecological goods and services.
- Tens of millions of people could be displaced in low-lying deltaic areas and small island states due to sea-level rise.

- There will be increased incidence of disease.
- The incidence of severe weather events will increase.

Many countries in sub-Saharan Africa have millions of people in abject poverty (per capita incomes of less than $1 per day), lack access to adequate food, clean water and modern energy, and rely on natural resources for their very existence. In some cases governments lack good governance and are faced with political instability, with some in conflict and others emerging from conflict. Hence, climate change, coupled with other stresses, risks local and regional conflict and migration, depending on social, economic and political circumstances.

Climate change is also an ethical and equity issue, with the most vulnerable countries being those who have contributed the least to greenhouse gas emissions historically. To a large degree there is an anti-correlation between countries with high per capita emissions and countries most vulnerable to climate change.

How to mitigate the risks of climate change

All major emitters of carbon dioxide and other greenhouse gases need a rapid and cost-effective transition to a low-carbon economy in both the production and use of energy and the management of forests and agricultural lands. In order to ensure food, water and human security, and protect the world's biodiversity, between now and the end of the century, the goal should be to limit the global average temperature rise to 2°C above pre-industrial levels – a goal endorsed in the Copenhagen Accord. This target should be recognised as a stretch target and, unless political will changes drastically in the near future and concerted action is taken, it is unlikely to be met. Therefore, we should be prepared to adapt to global temperature changes of 4°C, with unthinkable impacts.

Article 2 of the United Nations Convention on Climate Change requires:

> stabilization of greenhouse gas concentrations in the atmosphere at a level that would prevent dangerous anthropogenic interference with the climate system, and allow ecosystems to adapt naturally, ensure food production, and allow sustainable economic development.

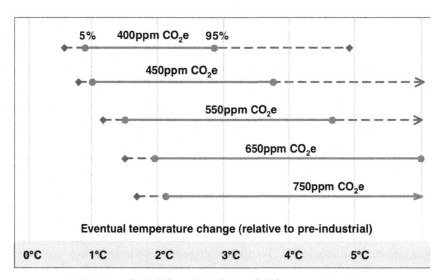

FIGURE 8.3 Probability of stabilising global mean surface temperatures as a function of greenhouse gas concentrations; taken from *Stern Review: the Economics of Climate Change* (2006, 294). The panel shows the range of temperatures projected at stabilisation levels between 400ppm and 750ppm CO_2 equivalent at equilibrium (CO_2e). The solid horizontal lines indicate the 5–95 per cent range based on selected climate sensitivity estimates.

So, key questions include whether to focus on physical or social outcomes, danger for all or danger for some, and who defines danger? Deciding what constitutes 'dangerous anthropogenic interference with the climate system' is a value judgement determined through socio-political processes informed by scientific, technical and socio-economic information.

The current level of greenhouse gases in the atmosphere, accounting for the offsetting effect of aerosols, is approximately between 380 and 400ppm CO_2e. Figure 8.3 shows the range of temperatures projected at stabilisation levels between 400ppm and 750ppm CO_2 equivalent at equilibrium. If we succeed in stabilising at between 400 and 450ppm CO_2e, there is a 50 per cent chance that global temperature changes will be limited to 2°C above pre-industrial levels, but with a 5 per cent probability of about 3°C. However, the likelihood of stabilising at this level is low unless concerted global action is taken now. If we stabilise at 550ppm CO_2e, there is a 50 per cent chance that global temperature changes will be limited to about 3°C above pre-industrial levels, with a 5 per cent chance of about 5°C. And, if we stabilise at 650ppm CO_2e, which is the level many scientists and economists feel is inevitable because of the lack of action to reduce emissions to date, there is a 50 per cent chance that global temperature changes will be limited to about 4°C above pre-industrial levels, with a 5 per cent chance of about 6°C.

To stabilise at 450ppm CO_2e or lower, global emissions will need to peak around 2015, and certainly no later than 2020. OECD countries would need to reduce their carbon emissions by at least 80 per cent by 2050, and developing countries would also need to decrease their projected carbon emissions significantly over the same time period. Climate-change-resilient development must be equitable because historically most of the greenhouse gas emissions have come from developed countries.

Many people had assumed that an appropriate combination of technology and policy options could enable us to meet our stabilisation goals and mitigate climate change. We now recognise that mitigation will require a combination of pricing and technological mechanisms, as well as good policies and behavioural change, that is, pricing carbon emissions and understanding behavioural changes is critical. A range of cost-effective tools (policies, technologies and practices) is already available to start us on a path to stabilise greenhouse gases in the atmosphere at 500ppm CO_2e or less.

Technology use and transformation is needed to reduce emissions. Better use of available low-carbon technologies coupled with improved development, commercialisation and market penetration of emerging technologies is required. Examples include:

- Efficient energy production and use across sectors: power generation (e.g. re-powering inefficient coal plants and developing integrated gasification combined cycle (IGCC) power plants); transport (e.g. developing fuel cell cars; developing mass transit; and improving urban planning), buildings, and industries.
- Fuel shift: coal to gas.
- Renewable energy and fuels: wind power; solar PV and solar thermal; small- and large-scale hydropower; wave and tidal power; and bio-energy.

- Carbon capture and storage (CCS); Integrated Gasification Combined Cycle (IGCC): geological storage of CO_2 produced during electricity generation (e.g. IGCC–CCS).
- Nuclear fission: nuclear power.
- Energy storage and distribution technology (smart grid; chemical / physical).

Increased investment in low-carbon technologies such as carbon capture and storage, second- and third-generation biofuels and efficient photovoltaics is urgently needed.

In addition to transitioning to a low-carbon energy system, it is essential to recognise the potential of ecosystem-based mitigation. A portfolio of land-use management activities can contribute to the objectives of the United Nations Framework Convention on Climate Change (UNFCCC), United Nations Convention to Combat Desertification (UNCCD) and Limited Nations Convention on Biodiversity (UNCBD), including:

- protection of natural forest and peatland carbon stocks;
- sustainable management of forests;
- use of native assemblages of forest species in reforestation activities;
- sustainable wetland management and restoration of degraded wetlands;
- sustainable agricultural practices.

The IPCC Fourth Assessment Report showed that putting a price on carbon can lead to significant emission reductions. Pricing mechanisms include emissions trading, taxation and regulations across national, regional and global scales and across all sectors.

There is a range of policy instruments that can assist in the transition to a low-carbon economy, including: energy-pricing strategies and taxes, removing subsidies that increase greenhouse-gas emissions, internalising the social costs of environmental degradation, tradable emissions permits (domestic and global), voluntary programmes, regulatory programmes including energy-efficiency standards, incentives for use of new technologies during market build-up, and education and training such as product advisories and labels. These policies need to be augmented by an accelerated development of technologies, which requires intensified R&D by governments and the private sector.

Reducing the risks through adaptation

Mitigation is essential because there are physical, technological and behavioural limits to the amount of adaptation that we can achieve. There are physical limits to adaptation on small, low-lying islands and complex deltaic systems, technological limits to flood defences and behavioural limits to where people live and why. The more we mitigate, the less we will have to adapt. Nevertheless, we know that adaptation is essential and must be mainstreamed, particularly into sectoral and national economic planning in developing countries due to their heightened vulnerability to climate-change impacts.

The estimated costs of inaction related to climate change cover a huge range, but are expected to fall between tens and hundreds of billions of dollars annually in developing countries alone by 2050. Furthermore, a preliminary assessment shows that tens of billions of dollars per year of Overseas Development Assistance (ODA) and concessional finance investments are exposed to climate risks. Comprehensive project planning and additional investments to climate-proof development projects are required. Financial instruments are available, but funds flowing through them need to be substantially increased.

Figure 8.4 illustrates many of the key elements of an adaptation strategy, and emphasises the importance of good governance. Good governance mechanisms are required for delivery of adaptive responses, and society's self-organisation and distribution of costs and benefits in society are determined by governance.

Failure to adapt adequately to current climate variability and projected changes is a major impediment to poverty reduction. Most sectors are maladapted to current climate variability due to inappropriate subsidies, pricing and planning policies. Unless adaptation is recognised as part of the development process and integrated into development planning, ODA will be undermined. This requires a climate-risk-management approach that takes account of the threats and opportunities arising from both current and future climate variability in project design. This process must be country-driven and focus on national needs and local priorities.

FIGURE 8.4 Key elements of an adaptation strategy (taken from: Tompkins et al., 2005).

Adaptation will require a broad range of policies, practices, technologies and behavioural changes. Hard structures are often the instrument of choice when dealing with coastal erosion, storm surges or river flooding, but there is a range of ecosystem-based adaptation activities which should be considered, including:

- coastal defence through the maintenance and/or restoration of mangroves and other coastal wetlands to reduce coastal flooding and coastal erosion;
- sustainable management of upland wetlands and flood plains for maintenance of water flow and quality; and
- conservation and restoration of forests to stabilise land slopes and regulate water flows.

Equally there are ecosystem-based adaptation measures to decrease the vulnerability of forests and agricultural systems, including:

- establishment of diverse agro-forestry systems to cope with increased risk from changed climatic conditions; and
- conservation of agro-biodiversity to provide specific gene pools for crop and livestock adaptation to climate change.

Research will play a particularly important role in decreasing the vulnerability of the agricultural sector to human-induced climate change. There will be a need to: (i) address water-deficit problems, through, for example, improved drought-tolerant crops and irrigation technologies; (ii) improve the temperature tolerance of crops; (iii) combat new or emerging agricultural pests or diseases; (iv) address soil fertility, salinisation of soils and improved nutrient cycling; (v) reduce external and energy-intensive inputs; (vi) reduce GHG emissions while maintaining productivity; (vii) improve the nutritional quality of food; (viii) reduce post-harvest losses; and (ix) improve food safety.

It is important to note that there are financial, physical, technological and behavioural limits to adaptation that vary geographically and on socio-political-economic conditions. For example, there are physical limits to potential adaptation on small low-lying islands such as the Cayman Islands; there are behavioural and cultural constraints that influence where we live and why, for example, people whose families have always lived in a river valley or coastal region prone to flooding; there are technological limits to the flood defences that can be constructed, for while London for instance can be protected by the Thames barrier, such options are probably not possible in large deltaic areas such as Bangladesh; and there are certainly financial constraints for many developing countries.

Strengthening the science–policy framework

Strengthening the science–policy interface is also critical for reducing the risk of being 'taken by surprise' or of an inadvertent negative impact of climate change regulatory activities. National and international, coordinated and interdisciplinary research is a critical underpinning for informed policy formulation and implementation. There is an urgent need for strengthening the scientific and technological infrastructure in most developing countries. Independent, global expert assessments that encompass risk assessment and risk management, for example the IPCC, have proven to be a critical component of the science–policy interface. Such assessments must be policy-relevant rather than policy-prescriptive.

However, we need a more integrated assessment process that encompasses all environmental issues within the construct of sustainable economic growth and poverty alleviation – that is, climate change, stratospheric ozone depletion, loss of biodiversity and ecosystem services, water degradation and air pollution.

An emerging idea that would significantly strengthen the science–policy interface is an electronic, web-based system where peer-reviewed and grey literature on all aspects of climate change, biodiversity and ecosystem services, in the context of food, water, energy and human security, is up-loaded, critically reviewed and synthesised with previous information in as close to real time as possible. It would: (i) assess changes in the Earth's climate, biodiversity and ecosystem services; (ii) attribute observed changes to natural and human causes; (iii) assess plausible future changes; (iv) assess the impacts on ecological systems, socio-economic sectors and human health; (v) assess adaptation options (technological, policy and behavioural); (vi) assess mitigation options (technological, policy and behavioural); (vii) evaluate the economic and societal costs of inaction and action; and (viii) report on the regulatory and legal frameworks at the national, regional and global level that are relevant to global change. The information would address a range of spatial scales – global, regional and sub-regional and, where possible, national level.

Reducing the risks of climate change through a global regulatory framework

A suitable policy framework would facilitate the emergence of appropriate pricing and technological mechanisms. A voluntary agreement will not work. Instead, we need a long-term (e.g. 2030–2050), legally binding global regulatory framework that involves all major emitters, including the EU, Russia, the USA, China, Brazil and India. The agreement should allocate responsibilities in an equitable manner (recognising the principle of differentiated responsibilities) and should include immediate and intermediate targets that are differentiated. Global emissions need to be reduced by at least 50 per cent by 2050, with industrialised emissions being 60–80 per cent below 1990 levels by that time.

The framework should expand the range of eligible Clean Development Mechanism (CDM) activities to include avoided deforestation, green investment schemes and energy efficiency standards. Sectoral and programmatic approaches should be considered. Financing for developing countries, as agreed in Copenhagen and Cancun, for both mitigation and adaptation will be essential, as will capacity building and technology cooperation.

Conclusion

There is no doubt that the evidence for human-induced climate change is irrefutable. The world's leading scientists, many of whom have participated in the IPCC, overwhelmingly agree that what we're experiencing cannot be attributed to natural variation in the climate over time, but is due to human activities and that, if we do not act, climate change will continue apace with increasing droughts, floods and rising seas, leading to major damaging impacts to the natural world (loss of species and degradation of critical ecosystem services), the economy (loss of agricultural production) and society (displaced human populations).

To achieve poverty reduction and sustainable economic growth we need to mitigate climate change and reduce other aspects of environmental degradation. This requires climate-change-resilient development, which must consist of strategies to cost-effectively limit human-induced climate change and adapt to the projected impacts. To mitigate climate change we must minimise the emissions of greenhouse gases and transition to a low-carbon economy, while recognising that access to affordable energy in developing countries is a prerequisite for poverty alleviation and economic growth. To adapt, we must integrate current climate variability and projected climatic changes into sector and national economic planning while taking into consideration the aspirations of local communities.

There is no contradiction between limiting climate change and economic growth; indeed, the cost of mitigating climate change is less than the cost of inaction, if one takes the ethical position of not discounting future generations. Delaying action, moreover, can significantly increase costs. Climate change undermines development and the Millennium Development Goals. Efficient resource use (for example energy) saves money for businesses and households. A green economy will be a source of future employment and innovation.

An equitable and substantive post-Kyoto agreement is essential if the aspirational target of 2°C, which most countries agreed to in Copenhagen, is to be realised. Given the limited success at Copenhagen, 2010 is a critical year for the world's political leaders to unite in the fight against climate change. And given that 2010 is the year of biodiversity, this presents an opportunity to address the issue of biodiversity loss and its relationship with climate change. Strong and visionary political leadership will be essential. We must not allow the climate deniers to use the incident at the University of East Anglia or the mistakes in the IPCC report to distract us or derail the political will to safeguard the planet. Industrialised countries must demonstrate leadership, and provide developing countries with the technical and financial assistance promised in Copenhagen to reduce their greenhouse gas emissions, while at the same time addressing the critical issues of poverty and hunger.

Effective action needs stable and credible environmental policies that support the long-term shift to a low-carbon economy and the sustainable use of natural resources. We need not just a small improvement in resource efficiency, but a radical shift. Public and private sector decision-makers need to take a long-term multi-decadal perspective. We must make advances in science and technology, with the emphasis on interdisciplinary research. We must get the economics right; this includes eliminating perverse subsidies and internalising externalities.

The future is not preordained. There are cost-effective and equitable solutions to address issues such as climate change, but political will and moral leadership is needed. We can limit changes in the Earth's climate and manage ecosystems more sustainably, but the changes required in policies, practices and technologies are substantial and not currently underway.

References/Further reading

Climate Change 2007: The Physical Science Basis (2010) Working Group I Contribution to the Fourth Assessment Report of the IPCC. Cambridge University Press.

Climate Change 2007: Impacts, Adaptation and Vulnerability (2010) Working Group II Contribution to the Fourth Assessment Report of the IPCC, Cambridge University Press.

Climate Change 2007: Mitigation of Climate Change (2010) Working Group III Contribution to the Fourth Assessment Report of the IPCC, Cambridge University Press.

IAASTD (International Assessment of Agricultural Science and Technology for Development) (2008) *Agriculture at a Crossroads 2008: Global Report.* Washington, DC: Island Press.

IAASTD (2009) *Agriculture at a Crossroads 2008: Synthesis Report.* Washington, DC: Island Press.

Interlinkages between Biological Diversity and Climate Change (2003) Ad hoc Technical Expert Group on Biological Diversity and Climate Change. Montreal: Secretariat of the Convention on Biological Diversity.

'International Assessment by an Ad-hoc Group of Experts for the Convention on Biological Diversity on Climate Change and Biodiversity 2009'. CBD Technical Series no. 41.

IPCC (2002) *Climate Change and Biodiversity.* Technical Paper V. International Panel on Climate Change.

IPCC (2002) *Climate Change 2001: Synthesis Report.* New York: Cambridge University Press.

Millennium Ecosystem Assessment (2005) *Living Beyond Our Means – Natural Assets and Human Well-Being.* Statement from the Board of Directors.

Millennium Ecosystem Assessment (2005) *Ecosystems and Human Well-Being: Our Human Planet: Summary for Decision Makers.* Washington, DC: Island Press.

Millennium Ecosystem Assessment (2005) *Ecosystems and Human Well-Being: Synthesis.* Washington, DC: Island Press.

Millennium Ecosystem Assessment (2005) *Ecosystems and Human Well-Being:* Synthesis Reports on: (i) *Biodiversity;* (ii) *Desertification;* (iii) *Wetlands and Water;* (iv) *Marine and Coastal Ecosystems;* (v) *Health WHO;* and (vi) *Opportunities and Challenges for Business and Industry.* All published Washington, DC: Island Press.

Robert Watson

Stern, Nicholas (2007) *The Economics of Climate Change – the Stern Review.* Cambridge University Press.

Tomkins, E. L., Nicholson-Cole, S., Hurlston, L.-A., Boyd, E., Hodge, G. B., Clarke, J., Gray, G., Trotz, N. and Varlack, L. (2005) *Surviving Climate Change in Small Islands: A Guidebook.* Norwich: Tyndall Centre for Climate Change Research.

United Nations Environment Programme (2007) *The Global Environment Outlook, GEO 4: Environment for Development.* UNEP.

Notes on the contributors

Mark E. Bailey MBE is an astrophysicist and the Director of Armagh Observatory. He obtained his Ph.D. at the University of Edinburgh in 1978 with a thesis on the evolution of active galactic nuclei. In recent years his research has focused on areas closer to home: the dynamical evolution of comets, asteroids and meteoroid streams; solar system–terrestrial interrelationships; and aspects of the comet and asteroid impact hazard. The asteroid (4050), discovered in 1976 by C.-I. Lagerkvist, was named Mebailey in March 1990 for his work on the dynamics and origin of comets. He is the co-author of *The Origin of Comets* (1990).

Mary Beard is Professor of Classics in the University of Cambridge and Fellow of Newnham College. She is author of several books on ancient history and culture, including *The Roman Triumph* (2007), *Pompeii: The Life of a Roman Town* (2008) and *The Parthenon* (2010). She is currently working on a history of Roman laughter.

Tony Cox, since starting research in 1968, has published over 150 research papers and 30 reviews and evaluations on a range of topics in Atmospheric Chemistry. His main contributions to the understanding of the chemistry of the atmosphere is through studies of kinetics and mechanisms of atmospheric reactions. His work led to many new insights into the atmospheric oxidation of sulphur dioxide and volatile organic compounds, the formation of peroxyacetyl nitrate and the chemistry of alkoxy radicals, which are central to photochemical oxidant pollution. He has also demonstrated the formation of novel unstable halogen compounds which become significant at low atmospheric temperatures and play important roles in the chemistry of Antarctic ozone depletion. He has contributed to numerous international assessments of tropospheric chemistry and stratospheric ozone depletion.

Christopher Hood (www.christopherhood.net) is Gladstone Professor of Government and Fellow of All Souls College Oxford. Previously he was Professor of Public Administration and Public Policy at LSE and before that worked at the Universities of Sydney and Glasgow. More recently he was Director of ESRC's Public Services research programme (2004–10) and chair of the Nuffield Council on Bioethics working party on Medical Profiling and Online Medicine (2008–10). He has taught politics and public administration on three continents and published over twenty books. His chapter in this book reflects a long-standing interest in risk and blame-avoidance in government, which goes back over a decade to his 2001 book *The Government of Risk* (with Henry Rothstein and Robert Baldwin) and his inaugural lecture given in Oxford in 2001, and he has dealt with the issue at greater length in his book *The Blame Game* (2011).

John O'Doherty is currently the Thomas Mitchell Professor of Cognitive Neuroscience at Trinity College Dublin and Professor of Psychology at the California Institute of Technology (since 2004). His research is concerned with elucidating how the human brain is capable of making decisions under conditions of uncertainty. To achieve this he applies psychological, computational and economic theories to functional brain-imaging data, as well as assessing the patterns of impairment in human patients with certain kinds of brain damage or neurological disease. He obtained his undergraduate degree in Mathematics and Psychology at TCD (1996), and then completed a D.Phil. in Experimental Psychology at the University of Oxford (2001). He was a Research Fellow at the Wellcome Department of Imaging Neuroscience at University College London (2000–2004).

Michael Scott is currently the Moses and Mary Finley Fellow in Ancient History at Darwin College and an affiliated lecturer at the Faculty of Classics, Cambridge. He is the author of *From Democrats to Kings* (2009) and *Delphi and Olympia* (Cambridge, 2010). His research concentrates on the roles of material culture in ancient Greek and Roman society. In addition, he is actively engaged in broadening access to, and engagement with, the ancient world through school talks, guest-lecturing and writing for national and international newspapers and magazines, as well as presenting historical documentaries for TV in the UK, USA and Australia.

Layla Skinns is a Lecturer in Criminology at the Centre for Criminological Research, School of Law, University of Sheffield and formerly the Adrian Socio-Legal Research Fellow, Darwin College and Teaching Associate at the Institute of Criminology, University of Cambridge. She has conducted a wide range of research on topics such as crime prevention, drug users and the criminal justice system, restorative justice and, most recently, on policing in England, Ireland, Australia and the United States. She has also authored a number of scholarly publications, as well as policy reports aimed at a wider audience of criminal justice practitioners and policy-makers. These publications include a forthcoming book entitled *Police Custody: Governance, Legitimacy and Reform in the Criminal Justice Process* (2011).

David Spiegelhalter is Winton Professor of the Public Understanding of Risk at the University of Cambridge, and Senior Scientist in the MRC Biostatistics Unit. His background is in medical statistics, particularly the use of Bayesian methods in clinical trials, health technology assessment and drug safety. He led the statistical team in the Bristol Royal Infirmary Inquiry and also gave evidence to the Shipman Inquiry. In his post he leads a small team (UnderstandingUncertainty.org) which attempts to improve the way in which the quantitative aspects of risk and uncertainty are discussed in society. He works closely with the Millennium Mathematics Project in trying to bring risk and uncertainty into education. He gives many presentations to schools and others, advises organisations on risk communication, and is a regular newspaper columnist on current risk issues.

Robert Watson's career has evolved from research scientist at the Jet Propulsion Laboratory, California Institute of Technology, to a US Federal Government program manager/director at the National Aeronautics and Space Administration (NASA), to a scientific/policy adviser in the US Office of Science and Technology Policy (OSTP), White House, to a scientific adviser, manager and chief scientist at the World Bank, to a Chair of Environmental Sciences at the University of East Anglia, the Director for Strategic Direction for the Tyndall Centre, and Chief Scientific Adviser to the UK Department of Environment, Food and Rural Affairs. In parallel to his formal positions he has chaired, co-chaired or directed international scientific, technical and economic assessments of stratospheric ozone depletion, biodiversity/ecosystems (the GBA and MA), climate change (IPCC) and agricultural S&T (IAASTD). Professor Watson's areas of expertise include managing and coordinating national and international environmental programmes, research programmes and assessments; establishing science and environmental policies – specifically, advising governments and civil society on the policy implications of scientific information and policy options for action; and communicating scientific, technical and economic information to policy-makers. During the last twenty years he has received numerous national and international awards recognising his contributions to science and the science–policy interface, including in 2003, Honorary Companion of the Order of Saint Michael and Saint George from the UK.

Lucia Zedner is Professor of Criminal Justice in the Faculty of Law at Corpus Christi College and a member of the Centre of Criminology at the University of Oxford. She has held visiting fellowships at universities in Germany, Israel, America and Australia, where she is also a Conjoint Professor in the Law Faculty at the University of New South Wales, Sydney. Her work spans criminal justice, criminal law and penal theory, and she is especially interested in risk, security and terrorism. Her recent books include *Criminal Justice* (2004), *Crime and Security* (co-edited with Ben Goold, 2006) and *Security* (2009). She is now working, with Oxford colleague Professor Andrew Ashworth, on a project that explores pre-emptive state action, proliferating risk-prevention measures, and changing patterns of criminalisation. It aims to develop principles and values to guide and limit states in their use of coercive preventive powers against individual citizens.

Index

Index

law 121–3, 125–6
  Roman 104
  soft 81
leisure activities 26
Long Road Sixth Form College,
    Cambridge 8
low-carbon technology 171–2
  and ecosystem-based mitigation
    172
luck 92, 106
  philosophy of 88

Machiavelli, Niccolò 69
May Day demonstrations 70
media, the 6, 7, 8, 10–11, 117
medical events 25
Mellor, D. H. 1, 10
Menander 97
micromort 10, 24–6
Millennium Development Goals (UK)
    178
MMR 10
mobile phone masts 10

National Lottery 18
national security strategy (UK) 127
natural catastrophe 133–6
  See also asteroids; astronomy; risk and
    natural disaster
Near-Earth Objects (NEOs) 13, 144–52
  See also Edgeworth-Kuiper belt; Oort
    cloud; Shoemaker-Levy 9;
    Tunguska event
negativity bias 65–6
neuroeconomics 11, 34–9
New York City 114

Obama, Barack 10, 19
O'Doherty, John 7, 11, 34–57
Oort cloud 145
oracles 99
  of Apollo at Delphi 99
  of Astrampsychus 101–4
Overseas Development Assistance (ODA)
    173

perceived avoidable harm (PAH) 64
perceived responsibility (PR) 64
perception
  of harm 74
  of responsibility 74
  of risk 115–17
  See also risk assessment; risk
    sensitivity; risk and statistics
Poisson distribution 19
police 3, 4, 74, 119
Pompeii 85
Prat, Andrea 78
pre-buttal 72
probability 10, 17, 18–24, 90
  in ancient world 90–1, 103
  probability neglect 117
  representing probability 21–4
    frequency in population 22
    frequency out of 'possible futures'
      22
    graphical representation 22
    interactive animation 23
    numerical chances 22
    natural language 21
    numerical odds 22
    numerical probability 22
Protect and Survive campaign, 1970s
    (UK) 126
Purcell, Nicholas 92

Red Army Faction 112
regional resilience forums (UK) 127
reinforcement learning 47–9
reinforcers (positive and negative) 37–9
Rescorla, Robert 47
resources 133
  See also climate change; humankind
risk 3–7, 8, 88–9
  adaptive risk 111–12
  and the brain 11, 34–57
  and climate change 7, 13, 14, 159–78
  and counterterrorism 118–20
    risk to expectations 118
    reputational risks 118
    organisational risk 119

187

Printed in the United States
By Bookmasters